See Y   e

HOW TO OUTRUN ORDINARY
& ACHIEVE EXTRAORDINARY!

by Darryl Rosen

ISBN-13: 978-1497455566

First printing: 2014

D Rose & Associates
darryl@darrylrosen.com

http://darrylrosen.com

Dedication

To anyone trying to
outrun ordinary and achieve extraordinary.

Table of Contents

Author's Note!

You will notice as you read this book that I end each chapter with the phrase "That's just the way it works!" Actually, I have done this in all of the books I've written. I chose these words because I want to emphasize that the principles covered are conceptually straightforward and are extremely effective when put into practice.

Unfortunately, however, they're often lost in the shuffle of our other thoughts when we find ourselves in a situation in which we want to take our performance to the next level.

I guess that ending each chapter in this manner is also my way of getting in the last word!

That's just the way it works!

Acknowledgements

There are many people who have helped me bring this book to you, and I am deeply grateful for their input and support. There isn't enough space to mention them all individually, but I do want to give special thanks from the bottom of my heart to:

Kathy Chiu, Tim Benton, Aleesa Daley, Alissa Dewitt, Melissa Engel, Marcie Faust, Scott Friedlander, Danny Garcia, Lionel & Daniela Garcia, Alex Gold, Lori Harder, Heather Kampf, Miriam Laundry, Sheira MacKenzie, Mimi Noonan, Mark Schwartz and Yose Widjaja for sharing your inspiring stories of courage, ingenuity, persistence, perseverance and hope. Thank you!

Charlie Bernatowicz for creating the cover for this, my 6th book. You've done all my covers and, amazingly, always seem to capture what I'm thinking, even when I'm not entirely sure what I'm thinking. Thank you!

Kim Weiner – my editor. Yes, you read the 40,000 words within this book over and over and, according to my calculations, changed each of the 40,000 words over and over. For some reason, calling you an editor doesn't seem quite right. You brought my writing to life. I know that because my words and thoughts came back sounding significantly better than my words and thoughts. Thank you!

Josh, Danny and Ben Rosen – my children. I'm never sure if you're laughing with me or at me. I suspect the latter but, nevertheless, I love you immensely. I've enjoyed sharing your stories with my readers. Thank you!

Jill Rosen – my wife. There is one reason I'm able to see my clients and write these books. YOU. You're the reason I get to tell these stories. You're the reason I get to do what I love. You're the reason I get to improve the lives of others. To quote my favorite line from a Barbra Streisand song: *You're exceptional. I can't wait for the rest of my life...*Thank you!

The Start

In 1989, I entered the Chicago Marathon and dropped out near the 14-mile mark.

In 1990, I entered the Chicago Marathon and…again dropped out near the 14-mile mark.

In what seemed like a bad dream (or full-blown nightmare), in 1991, I entered the Chicago Marathon and, yet again, made it nearly halfway…before dropping out at the 14-mile mark!

Who thinks I should have tried a half-marathon instead?

No! I was in tip-top physical shape. I should've been able to make it through the marathon.

The first year, I was a little embarrassed because all my friends and family were waiting for me at the finish line. I never got to see the wonderful signs they made for me. "Go, Darryl!" "You can do it, Darryl!" "Don't die, Darryl!"

The following year was humiliating. By then, my friends were having a field day with me. They'd say things like, "Hey Darryl, did you see that 9-year-old girl cross the finish line? What an inspiration! You should run with her next year!"

The third year was flat-out devastating. I recalled the story of Pheidippides, the Greek messenger who dropped dead after running *26.2* miles to announce victory in the Battle of Marathon. Why, I thought, couldn't he have died after *14* miles instead? That shorter distance would then have become the definition of a marathon!

After my third attempt, I resolved to never run again. I quit the sport in disgust and wrote a sad country song.

I'd *like* to say that the reason I failed to finish these three marathons was 60 MPH gale force winds or a fellow competitor stealing my shoelaces or spiking my Gatorade with a potent laxative…

…But it was nothing like that.

It was all in my head. I was mentally unable to *survive the middle miles* – the part of the race where the excitement of the start has faded and you can't yet imagine the glory of the finish line.

The *middle miles* are where the real race begins!

This is not a book solely about running, though I often use running examples to illustrate my points. It's really a book about success and achievement - a book about *outrunning ordinary and achieving extraordinary.* It's a book for those who want to change a few habits, as well as those who want to change the world.

In these pages, I'll share not only my stories, but also the stories of many remarkable people. In some cases, you'll be introduced to ordinary individuals who have achieved extraordinary goals (like my friend who is passionate about bringing fresh drinking water to third-world countries). In other cases, you'll meet people who excel in their areas of expertise but have faced and rebounded from seemingly insurmountable challenges (like the college track star who fell at a critical point during the Big Ten Championships yet still won her race). In all cases, the people you read about have the same overarching aspiration – to *survive the middle miles* in order to go somewhere special and attain worthwhile goals.

Will you have ever have to *survive the middle miles?* Of course! Anything worth having, doing or accomplishing forces you to spend some time in the middle miles. If you've ever set a goal and had to work hard to achieve it, then you know the feeling. Maybe it's wooing a new customer or spearheading your company's new initiative. Perhaps it's opening a new business, starting a new job, or working on an important project. To be successful with such endeavors, you have to get through the lean times. You might be pursuing a different type of goal, such a running a marathon or losing a few pounds. It doesn't matter, because what all these examples have in common is that the middle miles await you.

In the beginning of your endeavor, everybody is cheering. It's exciting. It's new. It might even be fun. As you work your way forward in time, though, the fun slowly dissipates. Interest and encouragement from the early supporters begin to wane. The problem in the middle miles is that it's too early to see the results that will occur with perseverance and patience. Many get disillusioned. Many get lonely, frustrated and aggravated. Some stop trying, or quit altogether - like I did in those three marathons.

Congratulations. By reading this far, you've shown the courage to start the race. Keep going, and the pages of this book will demonstrate what it takes to get where you're going in life. You'll learn how to *get back up* when you fall, how to *own your result* and how to *train your thoughts,* so that you have the best chance to *outrun ordinary and achieve extraordinary* results.

Those are just a few examples. It's going to be a great journey and you're going to make it to the finish line.

That's just the way it works!

Chapter 1. Act Like a Champion

In this first chapter, I'd like to highlight several individuals who exemplify what it means to "act like a champion." You don't have to win every race to be a champion, but always acting like a champion will help you *outrun ordinary and achieve extraordinary.* Much of this book will focus attention on you and your individual goals. Right here at the outset, though, I want to emphasize that part of acting like a champion is caring about others. You have to *want* them to win their individual races. In the heat of competition, true champions find a way to help others, even when it might risk diminishing the final score.

In this chapter, you'll hear the story of a decorated high school runner who learned a key lesson (the hard way) about the responsibility he had to his teammates. Then you'll meet a young lady who helped a fellow competitor in a high-stakes race in a way that will truly astound you. Finally, you'll meet my father, and I'll share the ways that he, throughout his career, ran a business of distinction while helping many others along the way.

Let's start with Scott Friedlander, the star of his high school cross country team, who with a little help from his coach, learned that the decisions you make for yourself affect more than just you.

Rewind to Scott's senior year, which could be described as "one for the ages!" He was coming off a cross country campaign where he won all sorts of races, broke records, and wound up earning all-state honors. He had become a cult celebrity in the Illinois cross country community and at his high school. From freshmen to seniors to faculty members, everyone knew him as "the runner." By October, Scott had gotten into the one and only college he applied to - Brown University. As Scott explained, "It was hard to imagine being any happier than I was at the time. I was on top of the world."

Scott had always prided himself on being a positive influence on others. He never abused the position of power he had earned as the captain and top runner on the team. He maintained his reserved personality and never tried to show dominance or tout his own ego. He had great respect for how the program had changed his life, and he tried to pay it forward the best that he could. Despite all his success and accolades, he was determined to be the same guy he had been his first three years in high school - the guy whose teammates were so important to him.

Nevertheless, he had changed a bit. "I had gotten cocky with my schoolwork," Scott shared. He slacked academically because he thought he had it all figured out. He didn't need to worry about high school because he had already gotten into the college of his choice. He figured all he had to do was maintain decent grades so that Brown University didn't rescind his acceptance. There was no reason to try any harder than that. As a result, he didn't study much for exams and earned a 60% on his first calculus test. Although he had never scored that low on an exam, it didn't bother him much because he figured he'd bring the grade up to an "acceptable" level before the end of the semester.

What he didn't count on was his coach being notified!

"I'll never forget that day. I was sitting in the lunchroom, as I did for over two hours every day. As part of my lack of academic interest, I had arranged my schedule such that my two free periods backed up to lunch. So instead of using my free time to do homework as I had in the past, I sat at the 'runners' lunch table for multiple hours as my teammates rolled in and out during their lunch periods. On that particular day, one of my senior teammates strolled into the lunchroom and said, 'Scott, the coach wants to see you in his office.'

"Coach took me to a small back room that was used primarily for tutoring, and there he unleashed on me. For a good five minutes (which seemed like an hour), he yelled at me. It was probably the first time anyone had raised a voice to me since I started high school. I was shocked and scared.

"The message he left me with was: You're being selfish. The team has given you a leadership position, but the effort you are giving is an example nobody should follow. You represent our program. Is this really how you want our program to be represented? Is this how you want your teammates to remember you?"

The coach's message that *your actions, while they may seem only to affect you, actually affect others* had never occurred to Scott. He's carried this lesson with him ever since.

Scott shared with me, "If you care about people and they care about you, then you represent them in the decisions you make. Whether that's your team, your family, or any group where there is a mutual desire to see each other succeed, your actions impact how the group is perceived." Scott took a lot of pride in the fact that the team consisted of a group of good kids who were extremely positive influences on each other. They did well in school and didn't get in trouble.

"We always heard about teachers and parents recommending the cross country team to 8th grade boys looking for an identity because of the positive, supportive culture we fostered. My academic decisions as a second-semester senior ran counter to that culture. I was not representing the team, a group I cared so much about, appropriately. When people thought of the runners, they thought of me, and I didn't want negative perceptions of me to be translated into negative perceptions of the squad. So, because of what Coach said to me, I changed my attitude."

Scott's grades improved, and even though it wasn't his best semester, his report card wasn't something that caused him shame. But more important than the grades was the fact that he acted like a champion.

Sure, he had to be reminded (by his coach), but he wasn't even 18 years old at the time. In the end, *it wasn't that he needed the message that mattered; it was what he did with the message.* He buckled down with his schoolwork (and leadership behavior) and set a better example.

Now more than five years later, Scott still comes to visit the team when he's in town. I know that the responsibility he feels to represent the team hasn't faded, despite the fact that he's out in the real world now.

"The bottom line," he told me, "is that I learned that when you make decisions, you need think about the people you influence and how your decisions will affect them. Your decisions reach much farther than you'd expect. I'm prouder of my last six weeks of high school than I am of all the prior experiences combined because of the legacy I left the younger runners."

Scott "acted like a champion" and he's continued to *outrun ordinary and achieve extraordin*ary in his life as a successful consultant. Meghan Vogel, also a runner, became a champion not for the race she won, but for the race in which she finished last.

Meghan had just won the mile run to become the 2012 Ohio State Champion for that event. A short time later that same day, while running the 2-mile race, she fell behind. What transpired after that is astonishing. As she struggled to narrow the distance by which she lagged the leaders, Meghan saw a fellow competitor struggle and fall to the track. Instead of focusing on her own performance, Meghan ran to the fallen runner, picked her up and guided her towards the finish line, which resulted in a last place finish for Meghan. Although Ohio High School Athletic Association rules would normally disqualify a runner for receiving assistance, in this instance, neither runner was disqualified. Take a moment to search the Internet for this video - it will bring a tear to your eye.

Many high school track and field championships take place in late May, when the weather can be either nastily cold or extraordinarily hot. The heat was oppressive that day and, according to the announcers, the other runner was overcome by heat. Nonchalantly, during the post-race interview, Meghan said, "I saw the girl needed help and I just figured I'd help her out. So that's what I did! I wanted to help the other runner cross the finish line. She worked hard to get here. She deserved to finish ahead of me!" Yes, as if the initial act of helping the girl up wasn't sportsmanship enough, Meghan made the conscious decision to push the other runner ahead of her.

When people talk about that day, they don't talk about the race in which Meghan finished first, they talk about the race in which she finished last. It's spellbinding how the humility oozes from this athlete. "She doesn't think what she did was terribly impressive," according to her father, but everyone else who watches the video would probably beg to differ. By demonstrating caring about someone else to this degree, Meghan truly acted like a champion and outran ordinary!

Scott and Meghan acted like champions at key defining moments in their lives. My father has acted like a champion day by day for his entire career. Talk about *outrunning ordinary and achieving extraordinary*…my father, Fred Rosen, built a successful business through hard work, people skills and caring for others. Drawing upon his experiences as a multi-sport high school and college athlete, he brought a champion's mentality to our family's retail business.

If you ask anybody who interacted with him, they'd tell you that he treated everyone with the utmost respect. He never belittled (either privately or publicly) any one of the many sales professional from vendors who would call on us. He knew that sales professionals had to put children through college, just like he did. If you needed a favor, you called my dad and considered it done. His word was as good as gold. As our business changed, he gracefully stepped aside and allowed others to do things he had always done so that they could develop needed skills. He was charitable and generous.

Often, a local sales pro would pay a visit with his or her national sales manager in tow. To be sure, it was an extremely important day for that sales pro. Dad was certain to make him or her look like a hero…always sure to point out at least one great thing the sales pro was doing to sell more products in our stores. He was a natural at making you feel like the most important person in the world to him at that moment.

He had a soft heart – I'd call it generous to a fault. As a company, when we cut back on employee loans, he still helped people out of his own pocket. He even loaned money to members of the community immediately surrounding our main store, which was in an economically depressed neighborhood. He never considered himself better than anybody else. The down-on-their-luck members of the neighborhood called him "Freddy," and he treated them with kindness. He may have accomplished more than they had, but he didn't consider himself any better than them. To this day, that's a lesson that has served me enormously well.

My father and I, our mutual goals were success and achievement for others, as well as ourselves. He taught me that success never happens without the help of others. To him, acting like a champion meant that you treat everybody with whom you come in contact with great dignity. That you never make people feel small or keep people waiting, a tactic some use as a display of power. He said the true mark of a champion is that you never consider yourself better than anybody else. That you always can have a kind word for people and let them feel proud of their lot in life.

One quick story before I conclude this chapter. Recently I attended a train-the-trainer program hosted by Jack Canfield. During the training, each day Jack would ask, "Who wants a standing ovation?" He'd offer this distinction to the first five people who came up on stage, but each day there were many more than five who volunteered. I watched this unfold with bewilderment. Why did people need this attention? What was I missing? I felt no need to take part, so I remained in the audience and clapped and cheered alongside my fellow attendees. The best I could figure was that these individuals needed some acknowledgment or encouragement. They needed approval of some sort, for whatever reason, and standing up there and soaking it all in helped them feel good in some way.

Guess what? These people live, work, play and travel among us. They're all over the place. Maybe it's the guy sitting next to me as I write this, waiting for a delayed flight! Or the young lady at Starbucks who served me my grande mocha frappuccino light this morning – and this afternoon. Or the young man unpacking boxes in the cereal aisle at your local supermarket. You get the drift…people who need your help, kindness, guidance and leadership are out there, but you won't see them with your eyes closed.

Scott Friedlander cared about his teammates, so he changed his ways. Meghan Vogel cared about a fellow competitor, so she gave a helping hand. My father spent 60 years helping others. You can do the same. Open your eyes wide and your heart wider. Care about others and you'll be labeled a champion, no matter what place you finish!

That's just the way it works!

Chapter 2. Dig Deep

One of my favorite things to do is search the Internet for videos of close track and field race finishes. Maybe I have too much time on my hands, but were it not for this hobby, I wouldn't have stumbled upon an epic duel between legendary British runner Steve Jones and a runner from Tanzania during a 10,000-meter race in 1983.

After watching the video several times, I began to contemplate the following questions:

> *Does it take more than strategy, training, preparation and a hint of determination to win a tight race? Does it also take courage? And, if so, how does courage, specifically, relate to success and achievement?*

It's pretty obvious that the most successful people are willing to pay the price in terms of hard work. Bruce Jenner, an Olympic gold medalist in the decathlon, certainly paid the price. He once said, "I've learned that the only way you're going to get anywhere in life is to work hard at it. Whether you're a musician, a writer, an athlete, or a businessman, there is no getting around it."

So is success all about *working hard*, or is it more than that? I firmly believe that it's more - that true success comes from the courage and the ability to *dig deep* when everything is on the line.

That's what happened in this amazing race.

A 10,000-meter race is almost 25 laps around a quarter-mile track. Steve Jones pushed the pace unmercifully for the first 23 laps. He built a sizable lead over the field, but he was getting caught with every stride. You could hear the resignation in the announcer's voice as he said, "Jones was looking for trouble and he found it." The Tanzanian runner was closing on him quickly, and it looked like there was enough real estate for him to pass Jones with plenty of room to spare. Despite running a very brave race, it appeared that Jones would have to settle for second place.

Jones seemed to be desperately trying to hold on to his lead, which was a tall order as he was thought to have very little closing speed. With 100 meters to go, the Tanzanian runner passed him. Apparently, it wasn't to be Jones's day. He must have been demoralized, leading for so long only to be passed with just a straightaway to go.

I know from firsthand experience, too many times to recall, what it feels like to be passed just before the finish!

Anybody who has ever competed in anything, whether on the playing field or in the workplace, knows how devastating it can be to hold the lead for so long and then be passed (literally or figuratively) at the last moment.

It's tough to come back from something like that.

It looked like a 2nd place finish was in store for Jones. I'm sure that's what everyone thought. Everybody except for Steve Jones himself!

He wasn't done yet – in fact, he was just getting started! In an act of what appeared to be overwhelming courage, he seemed to summon every bit of what was left in his reservoir and responded in grand fashion. He sprinted faster than anyone thought possible for him and won the race by a very slim margin!

The video of this finish is incredibly emotional and uplifting. It makes one wonder what exactly transpired in this competition. Was Jones's last gasp an act of courage? Does the word "courage" even have any place being used to describe a sport, or should it be reserved for wars and other more life-changing events?

Without question, going to battle or facing a catastrophic disease takes courage, but I also think that Jones displayed great courage in winning the race.

Here's why: Steve Jones undoubtedly had great coaching. Clearly, he also had enough raw talent, heart and determination to stay in the lead for so long.

However, that all pales in comparison to the courage it took for him to *dig deep* that day and to call upon the "extra gear"… the courage it took to go to a place he might never have gone before…a place he perhaps wasn't even sure existed.

Those who *outrun ordinary and achieve extraordinary* "dig deep." They accept the pain and discomfort that goes hand in hand with true achievement.

Do you have to *dig deep* to be successful?

Yes, while it takes heart and determination to make it to the finish line, the ability to dig deep is often the extra ingredient needed to outrun ordinary. Steve Jones and his 1983 victory is a great sports example, but there are numerous examples of people from all walks of life who need to "dig deep," some of them facing situations where the definition of success is survival. To illustrate, I'd like to introduce you to Alissa, an everyday person who went from the top to the bottom and is now working her way back up again.

These days, Alissa is an accomplished business owner. She started out her career by holding a number of corporate human resources positions, her last involving responsibility for a 10,000-employee organization. Things are great now, but there were some very dark times during the intervening years.

Alissa left corporate life to get married and start a family. With children on the way, she and her husband moved out of state expecting a promising future. Over time, though, problems arose in her marriage. As Alissa reflects, she admits that she allowed herself to stay in a state of limbo for a number of years in the hope of keeping her family together. As a result, she suffered a deep bout of depression and lost her way for a while.

The emotional state she was in also affected her health. Alissa shared with me, "I believe that many people hit rock bottom at some point in their life and often others don't know how severely they're suffering." In her case, she would find herself feeling the depths of despair late in the evenings.

Alissa made a decision that would change her life. She felt that in order to be the best possible mother to her children, her only option was to get herself out of "limbo" and to move out of state, closer to extended family where she knew she would find emotional support. While the thought of being near family was comforting, the concept of this move was still very scary because Alissa knew she'd have to re-build her life (personal and professional) from the ground up. In doing so, she went to a *place within herself that she never knew existed*.

That's what successful people do. They dig deep. They shift into another gear.

The journey wasn't an easy one, as Alissa spent four years as a single, homeschooling mother and struggling business owner. However, as she tells it, "It was being willing to step outside of deep seated fears and limiting beliefs that actually began the process of new victories and healed relationships."

Steve Jones dug deep within himself and won a medal. Alissa did the same and it may have saved her life. Those who *outrun ordinary and achieve extraordinary* dig deep and, in turn, see results.

I checked in with Alissa recently. Her consulting and coaching practice is growing rapidly, and her business was recently recognized by the State of Tennessee as a

Certified Woman Owned Business. Her vision of being a positive influence on companies and in the community has come to fruition, and she remains passionate about helping others achieve greater success in their lives.

Always remember, we all have the "extra gear" to call upon and the ability to reach places never imagined.

That's just the way it works!

Chapter 3. Dismiss the Doubts

In this book's introduction, I shared my marathon story, which took place from the late '80s to early '90s. You'll remember that it read like a Greek tragedy, starring me as the lead character - a misguided soul who dropped out of three straight Chicago Marathons near the 14-mile mark. When I tell this story, people inevitably ask, "Why didn't you try a half-marathon (13.1 miles)?" They ask that jokingly; however, what they're really asking is, "Did you train properly?"

My answer to the latter question is: ABSOLUTELY. The first year, my problem was simply starting out too fast. The memo on *pacing yourself* during races of this distance never reached my inbox. I must have looked like I was running the 100-yard-dash, the way I took off down Columbus Drive with reckless abandon that first year. Before long, the damage was done. The positive effects of my carbohydrate-loaded pasta dinner were gone, and all the muscle glycogen had turned into lactic acid – making it very hard to continue running.

My reason for dropping out of the next two marathons was less obvious to observers but so important that it will form the basis of our lesson this chapter. Simply stated, *I let the doubts take over*. I questioned my ability to finish the race, and the more I internalized that feeling, the harder it became to keep going. Soon, my legs felt as heavy as telephone poles, with each step more challenging than the one before it. If only I could have *dismissed the doubts*, I probably would have finished those two races.

Everyone has doubts in some form or fashion. However, those individuals who *outrun ordinary and achieve extraordinary* dismiss the doubts. By the way, it's not only laypeople who fall prey to this self-doubt, but also famous celebrities and experts in their field. Just this morning I was reading an article on *Yahoo's* website. Country singer Miranda Lambert related a story about approaching Carrie Underwood to do a duet with her.

"To me, this [was] such a big deal," Lambert told *People Country* about proposing the duet to Underwood. "It took me forever to write the email to ask her; like I was writing to someone I had a crush on and you don't want to mess it up."

It took a week for Underwood to respond — causing Lambert to fret to her husband that the former *American Idol* winner "probably hated the song" and was never going to talk to her again. Fortunately (for Lambert's peace of mind), Underwood eventually did reply, stating that the tune was "awesome."

The two singers set a date to meet in the studio to lay down the track. When that day arrived, Lambert was still feeling shaky about measuring up to the task. "When she came in the studio I was writing to my husband, 'I'm in over my head, I don't know what I've done!'" Miranda recalled. "When you respect someone like that, you get so nervous." Luckily, Lambert did manage to calm her nerves and record the song "Somethin' Bad," which turned out to be anything *but* bad!

Even a star that has won an American Country Music Award is susceptible to her inner doubting mechanism! If Lambert's level of insecurity had stayed high, her performance in the duet surely would have been compromised. That's just how the mind and body work.

Research in the field of kinesiology (the scientific study of human movement) has demonstrated a relationship between our thoughts and physical strength. The findings indicate that feelings of doubt and other types of negative thoughts often have a physically weakening affect on the body and lessen our ability to perform.

There is also support for the notion that positive

thoughts can have a positive effect on our ability to perform. An article published in *Medicine & Science in Sports & Exercise* highlights the impact of positive thinking by describing a study in which participants were put through cycling tests (to the point of exhaustion). The results of an initial test were considered the baseline. Half of the participants then underwent a two-week positive talk intervention while the other half (control group) received no special treatment. At the end of those two weeks, the cycling test was repeated.

The results? The positive self-talk group saw an 18% increase in endurance, while the control group showed no change. In addition, the positive self-talk group's perceived exertion (RPE) rose more slowly; the exercise at a given exertion level actually felt easier to them than it did

Thoughts affect performance much more than meets the eye.

to the control group.

In the Chicago marathons I attempted, my thoughts defeated me far more quickly than my level of fitness, nutrition, or strategy did. Whether my legs were actually getting weaker or whether I was *just thinking* my legs were getting weaker, I certainly wasn't using my thoughts to get me closer to the finisher's tent.

In the remainder of this chapter, I will present three strategies for dismissing your doubts.

Break the goal into manageable pieces

If Danny Garcia had focused solely on the magnitude of his task (finishing the 2012 Dairy Udderland Triathlon in Elkhart, Indiana), his already trying day would have become unbearable! He was competing in this grueling event on an unseasonably hot day. To be sure, when you sign up for a triathlon in the Midwest in August, you're rolling the dice on the weather, but on this day the dice would've melted. Danny's experience during the run quickly became less about time and more about survival as the day and the heat wore on.

Here's his story:

> I don't recall thinking about the heat or realizing how hot it was, but when I started the run, I felt

the thick, steamy air as soon as I hit the pavement. With the swimming and riding behind me (and more than 4 hours into the race), I faced nothing but open road. There was no shade, no clouds and no breeze; just the hot sun, 98-degree temperatures and an endless path of black asphalt ahead of me. I'm a positive guy but I have to say that every step was unbearable.

The only thing greater than my thirst for water was the intensity of my doubts. People were dropping like flies. Later I learned that there were a record number of athletes taken away in ambulances or seen in the medical tent. Not even half the competitors would finish. I remember thinking that this was almost *too hot to handle*. I had reservations about continuing and thought about throwing in the towel a number of times.

By mile five or six, I was "mentally" done. It was unlike anything I had ever experienced. I came very close to flagging down the dreaded "help vehicle" and hitching a ride to the finish line. I didn't even want my family outside in these conditions. I was riddled with doubt, and the emotions were draining my energy as much as the heat was.

Danny had arrived at a crossroads. He truly doubted whether he could continue running, but he also wanted to demonstrate to his daughter that anything is possible as long as you put your mind to it. So he hatched a plan: He would break the final miles into smaller, more manageable (almost bite-size) pieces. He explains, "In my determination, setting a goal of making it to the next water station was too much. It had to be more immediate. Make it to the spectator just up the road. Make it to the billboard just ahead on the left. Make it to the stop sign a few feet away. Keep moving forward."

Equally important, Danny actively congratulated himself for making it to these milestones. He went so far as to say out loud, "Great job, pal!" and "You're almost there, handsome!" It was a touch corny, yes, but extraordinarily helpful. Before Danny knew it, the next small milestone wasn't so small. It was the finish line. He finished second in his age group.

Though Danny's doubts intensified in the *heat of the battle* (pun intended), breaking his challenge down into manageable pieces helped him lessen his doubts and achieve his goal.

Toe the line - "Just do it!"

Yose Widjaja is a developer who specializes in the creation of mobile phone apps. In his field, an overabundance of doubt could prevent an idea from ever leaving the launching pad. Over-analyzing a project goal only intensifies doubt, so oftentimes, it's simply best to take action sooner rather than later.

My son, Ben, follows Yose's work in the mobile software industry and pointed him out as I was writing this chapter. Ben explained that developers like Yose compile hundreds of thousands of lines of code for a simple app. They also have to carefully consider the economics of their endeavor. Will it sell? Will it work? How will it be marketed? Ben asked an interesting question. "Wouldn't a developer like Yose need to dismiss his doubts quickly or run the risk of waiting so long that someone else *steals* the idea?"

I was intrigued, so Ben and I reached out to Yose and, despite the fact it was just past 1 a.m. in Australia, he answered our email quickly. "Sometimes," he explained, "You have to 'just do it,' to quote the famous expression!"

His best-selling product is Hipjot, a keyboard and note-taking application that eventually rose to be the #2 paid app in the productivity section of App Store. In the beginning, in order to dismiss the doubts, he spent some time thinking about what he wanted the app to do and how the keyboard algorithm would work. With pen and paper in hand, he moved away from the computer and sat on his sofa, diagramming keyboards, possible finger motions and how the algorithm would interpret them.

"It took me a while, but I eventually found a basis of the algorithm. Not a complete picture in my mind, but it was enough to convince me it *was* going to work. I spent a week implementing the base of the algorithm, and tested my theory that it'd be fast enough for a mobile phone to run. It turned out that my initial theory was a bit off (the app ran very slowly), but I was not *very* wrong. With a little bit of work, it'd run faster, I thought.

"And so the next few months were spent developing the keyboard. The keyboard algorithm itself took me a while to perfect, and required gathering much data for it to work as well as it does today. All the doubts I had eventually went away, as my understanding of the situation grew."

This brings us to Yose's previous point of "just doing it." You may not know much at first, but if you take the initial steps and keep moving forward, your understanding of the objective will grow, and the complexities (on which your doubts reside) will begin to feel more "solvable."

Of course, the decision to "just do it" requires some time investment, a firm belief in yourself and the conscious decision to get started in some positive way.

Jack Canfield talks about a similar concept in *The Success Principles.* He mentions what he and his business partner went through trying to market the first *Chicken Soup for the Soul* book.

> We were overwhelmed with possibilities and a little crazy. We didn't know where to start so we solicited the advice of a wonderful teacher named Ron Scolastico. He told us, "If you would go to a very large tree and take 5 swings at it with a very sharp ax, eventually, no matter how large the tree, it would have to come down." Out of that, we developed the *Rule of 5*, meaning every day we would do 5 things that would move us towards completion of our goal.

Moving forward in even a small way each day enabled Jack and his partner to *dismiss the doubts* and helped make the *Chicken Soup for the Soul* franchise what it is today. Imagine, on the other hand, if people like Yose and Jack Canfield let their inner critic take over...

...nothing would ever be accomplished.

Silence your inner critic

Newsflash! We're all born with a critic within us. Often, this critic sabotages our efforts. That was the case with Fran, a sales pro who desperately wanted to have greater financial success. I knew she could get there, but in order for that to occur, she'd have to take her inner sales critic to the woodshed.

Here's what I mean: Fran was her own biggest critic. She would hash and rehash every sales call, but the tone of her introspection was primarily negative. She had the skills to *outrun ordinary* but was never going to get there with her doubts wreaking havoc on her.

Earlier in this chapter, I explained that experts in kinesiology believe that doubts and negativity weaken the body. This was quickly becoming the case with Fran. She was taking off multiple work days per month and arriving at work late on other days; the stress of the job and revisiting all her failures was making her physically ill. Her symptoms weren't overly serious, but were enough to affect her performance at work.

It was important for Fran to understand that gaining information about past calls could be a positive, but only if she used that information productively. Fran, like most people, probably has around 35,000 thoughts per day, most of which are predominantly negative.

Her thoughts were akin to following: "I can't do this! I'm always screwing up! I'm never getting my point across! I'm worthless at this…"

Negative, negative, negative!

In fact, Fran would tell me that she beat herself up endlessly when a call didn't go her way. She could get downright mean to herself. So one day I asked her, "Fran, would you say these things to your children?"

"Of course not!" was her reply.

"Then why on Earth," I asked, "would you say (or think) that about yourself?"

I told Fran that *of course, it's ok to be introspective about your daily activities, but only from a standpoint of objective improvement.*

If your last sales call was a disaster, try to determine why. Could you have prepared more? Could you have been more enthusiastic about your product? Could you have presented more compelling sales materials?

Try to understand what happened; just don't go to town on yourself. If your introspection is raising more insecurities, then that's just more doubt you'll have to work to dismiss.

Instead, switch the conversation in your head to a less emotional discussion of improvement opportunities, and the experience will change from a negative one to a positive one.

As I will indicate in many parts of this book…doubt, negative self-talk and general pessimism are not all that uncommon. It's a regular part of *your* day and *my* day, and that's not going to change. What helps people like Danny and Yose and you and me *outrun ordinary and achieve extraordinary* is the ability to dismiss these doubts and keep moving forward. Once you get this habit down, you'll be unstoppable.

That's just the way it works!

Chapter 4. Dream

Many great people have tried to change the world. You know the names: Martin Luther King, Jr., Mahatma Gandhi, Steve Jobs…

These are a few of the biggies, the names you know. Under the radar, though, are names you don't know…yet. But they're out there – the names of people who are dreaming of making a difference, dreaming of a better way.

A few of them are profiled in this chapter. They're *outrunning ordinary and achieving extraordinary* in every sense of the word, every day of their lives. They're special because they want to dedicate their lives to causes that many people talk about, but few people actually do something about. Their dreams have shaped their goals and continue to fuel their efforts, every step of the way. We can learn much from their example.

Kathy Chiu

I met Kathy when she was working in the health services industry. She was unfulfilled in her career at the time, but she had great passion for a cause she was introduced to as a college student. This cause affected her so deeply it would bring her to tears whenever she thought about it. I was instantly impressed by her concern for people suffering halfway around the world. Here's her story.

Kathy relates:

> I was 21 years old when I realized how big the world is and what problems really matter. I had made the decision to study abroad for the month of June 2009 in Tanzania because that program offered the classes I needed to graduate.
>
> While I was in Tanzania, every day I saw women and children walking to procure water. Many of the women and even some of the children carried infants on their backs, along with dirty plastic jugs in which to collect the water. It was heartbreaking. Our class traveled from place to place on a van, and whenever we passed women and children walking for water, we stopped to give them the water that we had.
>
> I'd think to myself - what do you mean they don't have water to drink? Is this real? How is it possible that they don't have access to safe drinking water in their home? I was shocked. I was ashamed of myself and of my fellow New

Yorkers. I felt this way because I knew how often New Yorkers took for granted this natural resource that isn't accessible to so many other people throughout the world. I didn't feel like I had the right to access clean water at the tip of my finger. I couldn't imagine how people less fortunate than me suffered emotionally when their infants got sick from drinking dirty water and the question they wondered was "Will my child survive the next day?"

I felt horrible and disgusted. I was so angry with myself and nearly everyone in the world for not taking care of the people who didn't have clean water – a basic necessity for life.

Even when I returned to school after my time in Tanzania, the images and feelings never left me. I was obsessed with the struggle of the women and children I witnessed, and I soon began looking for organizations that provided appropriate water solutions.

I learned of a student organization called the Global Water Brigades (GWB) and almost immediately felt compelled to start a chapter at my university. I wanted more students to be aware of the global water crisis. I wasn't going to sit idly by, and I felt that if I brought this organization to my university we could change the lives of many people. I knew that if we worked together, we could give more people around the world access to safe drinking water. The more students that could be inspired to take action, the more the situation would improve.

Helping people in these nations became my *reason for being*! Whenever I had the chance to talk about my time in Tanzania and the clean water issue, I did. Then, when I had the opportunity to help address this same problem in Nicaragua, I went there. I had decided that my overarching dream in life was to do something meaningful for the world and for the survival of the human species. I would accomplish this by bringing clean water to more people and by working to create sustainable communities in developing nations.

The mental images of women and children walking miles and miles each day for water occupied Kathy's mind back then, and they still do to this day. Who knows…her passion for these people is so strong that she might even win the Nobel Peace Prize one day!

Marcie Faust

Marcie has far-reaching dreams, as well. As a teacher at a middle school in suburban Chicago, Marcie's philosophy is that it's a *teacher's responsibility to transform the next generation.* She believes in thinking big and feels that every teacher should make a difference. She relishes the opportunity to help her students build the skills necessary to handle the challenges they'll face in the future.

Marcie favors a somewhat untraditional teaching approach that encourages experimentation. This unconventional thinking created some challenges at the beginning of her career.

As she tells it:

> During my first year teaching, I had many families who didn't feel comfortable with some of the things that I was doing in my classroom. I was young, idealistic, and an out-of-the-box thinker. I didn't believe in doing things the way they had always been done, and this frustrated some of the parents.
>
> One of my students, the youngest of three, was virtually failing all of her math tests. I could tell

that her mom was tough on her, and that she didn't believe in me as her daughter's teacher. The student told me, "My mom thinks that you're a terrible teacher, but I told her that you're the best teacher I have ever had. You're the only one who believes in me."

I'll never forget her comment. It was exactly the reason why I pursued education as my career. My dream wasn't to appease the parents, it was to build self-esteem in their children; to build them up and see their unique qualities so they would believe in themselves.

I suppose the parent's criticism motivated me to work harder and prove that I was not just a good teacher, but also a great one. The truth is, I'm really no different than I was 10 years ago. Sure, I am older and because I have kids of my own, my perspective has broadened, but I'm still idealistic and an out-of-the-box thinker. I'm an innovative educator, always willing to be the first to try something, even if it fails. That's something that my students all know about me. It's what they deserve and what they'll remember.

Over the years, all three of my boys had Marcie as a teacher, so our family (like many others) knows of her skills as an educator. However, her reputation goes beyond our local community. In 2011, Marcie was among six educators selected to appear in a Sprint Technology ad campaign. She was chosen, in part, for her pioneering and innovative use of technology in the classroom. It's an honor for which she is extremely proud, because it reinforces her belief in pushing the envelope with her students.

Sheira MacKenzie

Kathy and Marcie's dreams were crystallized early on in their lives. Sheira's dream, in contrast, didn't materialize until she was close to middle-aged. As is often the case with inspirational leaders, Sheira's path wasn't initially clearly defined. It took her a while to find her focus. She battled addiction and was just a shell of her amazing self for many years. It wasn't until she recognized her inner strength and what she was capable of that her dream of empowering women to find their unique purpose came to fruition.

Her story is a compelling reminder that people can find their calling and define their dreams at any time in life.

Born the children of missionaries, Sheira and her brother moved around quite a bit – even spending several years in Central America. It was a tough upbringing financially. While her parents had their faith (which made them happy absent financial means), Sheira went without many of the *trappings* that her friends enjoyed.

I could hear the emotion in her voice as she explained to me:

> My mother made my clothes. It was embarrassing. It wasn't that I needed fancy clothes; I just wanted to fit in. I wanted to participate in the activities that other kids enjoyed, but our religious beliefs prevented that. As a result, when I got older, I became a magnet for material stuff. It was like a race with no finish line. Get a big job. Get lots of money. Get lots of stuff. It was like I was making up for lost time – but I wasn't happy.
>
> When I turned 21, my genetic disposition to alcoholism kicked in. I could party and have the immediate gratification of being what other people wanted me to be. With a glass (or bottle) of pinot grigio in my hand, I'd find a plethora of external factors that seemed to validate who I was…

...But I wasn't validated at all; I was sad and empty.

Even in the depths of despair, Sheira showed little sparks of spirit, and there were temporary periods in her life where she would shine and enjoy a certain level of success. These were times when she would feel whole and financially secure, but eventually she would drink or spend her savings away. She was her own best saboteur, and along the way, she burned bridges with friends and family. She couldn't get out of her own way.

It got to the point where her life was unmanageable.

I was exhausted from trying to keep up the pretense of who the world thought I was...from the train wreck I was behind the scenes. I knew that there was a loving, responsible, self-caring person underneath all the layers of self-sabotage...but I just couldn't seem to imagine a world without alcohol in it. I had been seeing a therapist for six months who was young, vibrant and, unbeknownst to me...also in recovery. One day, after a 24-hour binge (and driving in a blackout), I went to our session and just broke down. I had no idea that she was in Alcoholics

Anonymous, as we'd never discussed my drinking. She just knew.

Sheira went to her first AA meeting that night and never looked back.

She fully embraced the program, followed the steps set before her and did what she was told. She credits the program and her faith for helping her turn off the switch in her head and eliminate the need for alcohol. She became sober in 2003.

After addressing her addiction, Sheira found that underneath all her sadness was a spiritual foundation. But the situation was still difficult. She had lost all her friends. She had no professional career. However, she persevered, and now, ten years later, things are vastly different.

Sheira is sober, married, successful in business, and helping to raise her two stepchildren. Moreover, her dream has taken root and she's found the inner light that used to show up only on occasion. As she explains it, "My life purpose is one of service. It's not about stuff; it's about sharing with others what has been given to me."

Specifically, Sheira's dream is to help other women discover their unique purpose so they can find happiness independent of material possessions. She knows that there are others who struggle like she did, so she strives to help them believe in their potential. To help them build a deep confidence that they have the abilities, the inner resources and the skills to achieve their goals.

It turned out that Sheira possessed this type of belief in herself all along, but it was buried. With a warm, self-effacing charm, she told me, "I love where I am now. Love it! But, man, it took a long time to get here. I didn't take the short route. Sure, it was fun at times, but if I could do it again, I'd arrive at this amazing place a little bit quicker!"

She believes that "believing in yourself is a choice." As she talks to women trying to find their purpose in life, she lets them know that "the past is the past!" Sheira makes the point that the past affects us but doesn't define us. For many years, she lamented her childhood, but over time she came to realize that her parents had given her a wonderful spirit.

Her dream is to help others bring their unique spirit to the surface.

I profiled her in this book to show that it's never too late to make a difference. Sheira got a late start but through her extraordinary efforts, she is making up for lost time. She talks extensively with people overcoming what she calls "hurts, habits and hang-ups." Everywhere, even the local beauty salon, is fertile ground for her message! She's an equal opportunity inspiration-giver!

Kathy's vision of clean drinking water for all, Marcie's creative approach to developing our children and Sheira's inspirational ways of helping others find their purpose in life - all involve dreams of a better tomorrow. People with dreams such as these are outrunning ordinary in the race towards improvement for society overall. Their stories are powerful reminders of the good that can come from acting upon our grandest dreams.

That's just the way it works!

Chapter 5. Embrace the Race

Our first run together was to the local Dairy Queen. Truth be told, it wasn't as much a run as it was a shuffle or a brisk walk. It certainly wasn't pretty. This initial run took place on the day my dad announced *it was time for him to quit smoking and get in shape.* I later found out that it was my mom who told him *it was time to quit smoking and get in shape.*

In a bit of delicious irony, ice cream was the incentive that evening. When my dad and I arrived at the Dairy Queen, we ordered hot fudge sundaes and called Mom for a ride home.

I was hooked! Not on Dairy Queen, but running. Well, both, actually.

The next year when I turned 13, my dad and I decided to enter the Chicago marathon.

Many of my 7th grade classmates thought this was quite funny. They didn't think I could do it. They doubted me because I was small, skinny and somewhat un-athletic.

They were the naysayers and, boy, could they be nasty.

"You can't run that far."

"Your time will suck."

"You're not fast enough."

"So and so is doing it. He'll kick your butt."

"So and so" was a classmate who had also entered the marathon and was thought to be a much more capable athlete.

These comments were not just hurtful; they also caused me to doubt myself. I didn't really understand at the time, though, that I was letting the words affect me in this way.

As my doubts intensified, I was racked with indecision. A father/son event that was supposed to be a rewarding bonding experience wasn't yielding any rewards, only consternation. Finally, after much deliberation, I told my dad I was dropping my plans to run the marathon. I said that I thought (based on what I had been told, and what I was now telling myself) that it wasn't going to be possible for me to finish the race. Maybe the goal was too ambitious.

My dad wouldn't hear of it. As a former college athlete, he knew a thing or two about success in athletics. Instead of getting on a soapbox, he simply pulled out his stack of *Runner's World* magazines. In the marathon issue was the famous quote by Napoleon Hill, author of the widely-known success manual *Think and Grow Rich.* Dad read the quote to me:

"Whatever the mind can conceive – the mind can achieve…"

So, my dad reasoned, if I believed it was possible for me to finish the race, it could be done. I would find my way to the finish line. However, if I envisioned myself leaving the race sans a finisher's medal, then that's exactly what would happen. He threw all sorts of motivation at me that day. Another gem was *"If you think you can, or you think you can't – you're right."*

Sometimes you have to just "Toe the Line" and take action!

Through his guidance I learned that you can't *outrun*

ordinary and achieve extraordinary if you don't embrace the race. You must believe that it's possible. So I *abandoned* my plans to *abandon* the race, and my dad and I sent our applications in that very evening. I think he was in a rush to cement our participation before I changed my mind again.

Embrace the race!

Neuropsychologists who study expectancy theory point out that we spend our whole lives becoming conditioned. Our brains actually learn what to expect next; furthermore, when our brain expects something to happen a certain

The longer you believe something, the harder it is to change!

way, we often achieve exactly what we anticipate!

That's why it's so important to hold positive expectations.

The subconscious responds similarly to fantasy and reality. Therefore, if your conscious thoughts are laced with images of the glory of the finish line, your subconscious will think, *"I can go with that. Let's do it. We can get it done."*

On the other hand, if your thoughts are polluted with a hodge-podge of limiting beliefs, you won't achieve your goals. In many cases, it's just that simple.

It also helps to have someone who believes in you. My dad believed that both of us could complete the marathon. His belief that I could succeed meant a lot to me. I'm not sure why he felt that way, given the fact the neither of us really knew anything about marathon running. Maybe it was machismo or bravado but it really didn't matter. I started to believe I could do it because someone close to me was in my corner. Whenever doubt reared its ugly presence, my dad kept us moving forward – both literally and figuratively.

So *embrace the race* but, while you're at it, find someone who supports your efforts. Surround yourself with people who believe in you. In my career, I've learned that many of the naysayers are just jealous. They would rather tell you why something isn't possible, rather than brainstorm ways to make it work.

Also, when you have the opportunity to provide support to others, carefully consider how you do it. I remember the story of a sales professional who wanted to become a manager in his company. His direct supervisor, instead of helping the sales professional devise a plan for reaching management over time, felt a better play was telling him that *"it would never happen!"*

The sales professional was heartbroken and left the company a short time later.

This manager was way out of line. Rather than dousing the young man's ambition with a fire hose, he should have listed three or four ways the professional could improve in order to be eligible for the promotion he coveted. The manager had no right to predict the future. He should not have assumed that the sales professional wouldn't do what was necessary. It wasn't his place to decide if the young guy was hungry enough, or whether he would take the required steps. As long as the goal was reasonable, the sales professional was entitled to the support.

Yes, the goal must be reasonable. For example, you can't possibly drop 100 pounds safely in two months, so don't expect your subconscious to figure that out for you. Becoming a millionaire overnight after bankruptcy isn't going to happen, either. Further, I can think all I want about a super-fast race time; however, if I'm doing all my training runs at a snail's pace, all the positive thinking in the world isn't going to make me any faster. So there has to be some logic or else you're just setting yourself up for disappointment.

Aubrey Daniels, in his book, *Oops! 13 Management Practices That Waste Time and Money*, suggests that when individuals repeatedly fail to reach goals their performance declines. Dropping ten pounds in 3 months, for example, is a more effective way to approach weight loss.

Regarding that first marathon as a wiry thirteen year old, once I shifted my thinking, both my training and mindset improved. I focused on my determination to use all means at my disposal to finish the race, and I saw that possibility as real. That's the tenor of thought that helped me.

So *embrace the race* and believe it's possible. I finished the 1979 Chicago Marathon on a brutally hot day. It was slow - really slow - and extraordinarily painful. I suspect the race winner had a good long shower and a meal before I found the finish line. Perhaps he had already flown home! None of that, though, was of any concern to me. I was proud to have finished and felt great wearing my race t-shirt the next day for all my friends to see.

So embrace whatever type of "race" you're in – be it physical, professional or personal in nature. Believe that you can make it to the finish line! This outlook will propel you towards your goals.

That's just the way it works!

Chapter 6. Exercise Your Voice

Have you ever watched a competitive running event in person? It's pretty thrilling for runners and non-runners alike to see so many people laying it all on the line in pursuit of a special goal or achievement. I have always found it very inspiring. If you've ever witnessed such a race, you've probably noticed that many runners write their names on their T-shirts. Why, you might ask, would they deface an article of clothing with a magic marker?

The reason runners personalize their race-day clothing is so strangers in the crowd will cheer for them and call out their names. Many running publications suggest this as a way to heighten and enjoy the race-day experience. As you know by now, I've run my fair share of races and have on many occasions run alongside people who decorated their clothing in this way. They seemed to feed off the energy coming from the crowds. The simple sound of hearing names called can motivate tired runners as they battle towards the finish line.

Runners who do this are *asking* for cheers from an adoring crowd. They're **exercising their voice.** They're asking for the support they need to reach their goals – in this case the finish line. Similarly, your efforts to *outrun* *ordinary and achieve extraordinary* should include an element of asking for help. Asking for guidance, asking for what you need in order to be successful…or, in the example I'll use to illustrate this key to success, asking for what you need to get through one of those "hot" yoga classes!

My wife, Jill, loves yoga and was thrilled to find a "hot yoga" studio during our vacation in Florida. Since she'd never been to this studio before, she didn't know she needed to bring her own towel.

"I have a problem, they have no towels here" is what she texted me right after I dropped her off at the studio.

I was surprised to learn after picking her up that she *could* have had a towel for the ghastly sum of $2 – if she'd had her wallet AND asked for the towel.

Yet she didn't ask. *"It's no big deal,"* she reasoned. *"I knew I'd survive. I've been married to you for 22 years, after all."*

Even after pushing that hurtful comment aside, I remained a bit perplexed and asked, "Why didn't you explain your situation - that you're from out of town and that you could pay the $2 tomorrow or when your husband picks you up?"

All she needed to say was, *"Hi, I'm from out of town. I didn't realize I had to bring my own towel. Could you spare one?"*

I think they'd have handed one over even without charging her.

We'll never know, but what surprises me about this situation is that Jill isn't afraid to ask for anything else. (Do you know anyone who orders a beet salad without the beets, add avocado?)

Nobody does it alone

Nobody achieves success without the help of others. Describing someone as "self-made" isn't really accurate. Steve Jobs had help along the way. Jill's favorite rocker Bon Jovi had help – a New Jersey radio station that took a chance on his music. Successful people ask and they ask and they ask, and before long, people are asking them. Many of us, at some point in our lives, have probably asked someone to take a chance on us or to help us.

But many others don't ask for what they want and for what they need to be successful. And because they don't *exercise their voice*, they don't realize their true potential.

Why people don't ask

Experts theorize that people avoid asking due to fear.

The fear of looking stupid - because you're supposed to have all the answers.

The fear of embarrassment - because you're supposed to have all the answers.

The fear of feeling powerless - once again, because you're supposed to have all the answers.

Don't forget about the fear of feeling vulnerable and the fear of repercussions. Pride can get in the way, as well. Maybe you grew up in a house where "you just did as you were told!" A buddy of mine remembers his father always saying, "Don't question me," and this message wasn't conveyed with a smile.

I had a young sales professional tell me that he doesn't ask because of the perceived risk. He fears for his job security if he appears not to have all the answers.

Whatever the reason, many people just don't ask – but often you won't get what you want without asking.

In fact, there was an interesting experiment conducted years ago in New York City. A young woman entered a cafeteria, placed her suitcase by a table where another person was eating and went off to get some food. While she was away, a young man came by, picked up her bag and walked off with it. In only **one** out of eight trials did the fellow diner at the table make an effort to stop the "suitcase thief."

However, when the same woman entered the same cafeteria and placed her bag down where someone else was sitting, **and then asked that person** *to keep an eye on it* while she got some food, her tablemate stopped the "thief" EVERY SINGLE TIME.

The same experiment was replicated at a nearby beach with the exact same results.

The moral: When you ask, people will usually come through for you.

How to ask

For this, we'll turn to a fantastic book on the subject of "asking" called *The Aladdin Factor.* The most important variable is creating and communicating an expectation of success no matter what you're asking.

1) Ask with the expectation that you'll get it

Increase your level of conviction that you'll receive the support that you ask for. If your expectation is positive, that will affect everything else: your posture, your eye contact, your tone of voice and your choice of words. You'll come across as someone who is extraordinarily confident - someone to whom others would love to say, "YES."

Example: Please don't tell the people at Hertz, but whenever I bring one of their cars back a few hours late, I march right over to the Gold Desk and ask them to take the extra charges off. It's how I ask, I believe, that makes the difference. I've seen people try the same thing with less success. They usually ask, in an unsure tone, "Could you do me a favor, can you take the extra time off?" The answer, most often, is "no!" It's almost as if my fellow travelers expect a negative response and that's what they get. I ask with more confidence. I say, "I'm a little late because I was fueling the car up. Please make sure to charge me for just one day. I love renting from Hertz!" It works every time! When I ask in this manner, I'm asking with a positive expectation, conviction and the thought that I'll get the response I desire.

Another example: A friend of mine, Leslie, was starting the job of her dreams. In order to complete a project in an exemplary manner, she felt the need to gather a few bits of additional information from her department head.

There were two ways she could have asked for this. The first way was to question whether she could have (or was entitled to) such information. The second way was to act "as if" it was just a matter of **how** she could get the information she needed. Instead of saying, "Could I have some additional information?" she said, "What's the best way for me to get this information - quickly?" She was successful in this effort because she assumed that the delivery of such information was purely a logistical matter.

It takes a bit of hubris to be successful with your requests, but all the audacity in the world won't help if you don't ask the right person, which leads me to my next point!

2) *Ask someone who can give it to you*

Direct your request to someone who can help you. Though this may seem like an obvious statement, this is where it pays to do your due diligence. Find out who is really *pulling the strings*. Make sure you are climbing the right tree. Going back to the Hertz example above, a lesson I learned early on in my travels was to ask someone other than the guy checking in the cars. I quickly realized that he's busy with the cars being returned and has no authority to modify my rental charges. Talking his ear off would just cause me to miss my flight. Now I go straight to the Gold Desk.

In sales, it's imperative to speak to the decision-maker. Many sales professionals won't visit accounts when the decision-maker is present because they find that dealing with that individual is too intimidating. So, instead of going out on a limb, these otherwise assertive professionals will invent every reason under the sun to visit on a different day. Then they wonder why they don't succeed in that account.

3) *Be clear and precise*

Stipulate exactly what you want. When returning a car late, don't say, "Can you help me out here?" Clearly state what you want to happen. Say, "Please remove the charge from my account." Be explicit with your request - not rude and demanding, just clear and targeted. The very act of eliminating the need for someone to contemplate *what to do* will make it easier for him or her to comply.

I remember from my days as a beverage retailer when sales professionals would come and ask for *favors*. They wanted us to buy something to help them out. Many of these individuals would satisfy the two criteria above:

They'd ask with a positive expectation and, because they were asking me, they were asking the right person.

Then it got hazier. Some of the requests were clear and some not so clear. Sales pro "A" would say, "Can you help me out?" I would normally say "no" because the statement was just too vague and I had enough inventory! Plus, I wasn't sure what type of help he wanted, so I took the easy way out. Sales pro "B" was more specific. He would say, "Can you buy *this* much product and can you build *this* type of display?" It's not that I'd agree at once to this request, but at least I had a starting point if I was interested in considering it.

In a perfect world, those around you would know exactly what type of support you need to be successful, but we don't live in a perfect world. So *exercise your voice* and ask for it. Even if once in a blue moon your request is denied, you're no worse off than before.

If you want to *outrun ordinary and achieve extraordinary,* you can't go it alone!

That's just the way it works!

Chapter 7. Get Back Up

Most high-caliber athletes would simply have walked off the track. Lying face-down on the track's surface, they wouldn't have had the resolve to continue. The decision would have been swift and based on the thought "I'm out of it. There is no way I'm going to catch up to those other runners with only 200 meters to go."

But this is <u>not</u> what transpired when Heather Kampf found herself in this situation dreaded by every competitive runner. In mere seconds, she lived out one of my most important success principles.

Get back up...

Heather was a decorated high school track and field star from Minnesota, and in 2008 she was living out her dream of competing for her state university. She had helped her team win the previous year's Big Ten Indoor Track and Field title by individually scoring 23 points, a feat which can only be accomplished by performing amazingly well in many events. Buoyed by their success in 2007, Heather and her teammates wanted to achieve even more in the 2008 competition.

With that goal in mind, Heather toed the line for the 600-meter dash, which was scheduled to start just 40 minutes after her previous race. The 600 is a race that's quick and unforgiving; it feels like it's over before it even begins! Heather was the pre-race favorite and her team was counting on her. The first two laps were rather uneventful and with one lap to go, she was in prime position to break the tape and bring home the trophy.

Then she tripped.

Heather thinks a runner stepped on one foot, then her other foot, and in short order…

…She was face planted on the track, at the feet of the other runners who were trying to avoid placing their spikes on her head. (An unpleasant outcome for many reasons, including the fact that she already had her ears pierced.)

Her goal of being "a machine for the team" was seemingly as out of reach as the three girls she was chasing. When we spoke, she reflected that the "fall happened so quickly that it didn't seem particularly treacherous. It was only later when her dad showed her the video…

…That she realized how bad it actually was.

But back in the moment she thought, "Get back up. I need to earn points for the team."

She got up and gave chase. Slowly but surely she began to believe the impossible could be possible. One girl was in sight. Pass! Just two more to go - her teammate and a rival from another school. Suddenly, she realized, "I'm not that far back!"

She kept going. "When I race," Heather told me, "I hardly identify who is who, rather they are all just bodies, targets to try to catch before all is said and done."

The targets were in sight and the race was far from determined…

As the home crowd ushered her in, Heather took long strides to out-lean both ladies at the tape. The last girl she passed was her teammate. Heather was thrilled with her points earned and 1st place finish in her heat. In addition, she was extraordinarily pleased that her young teammate also did well.

Due to the combined efforts of Heather and her Minnesota Gopher teammates, the Big 10 trophy again went to Minnesota!

Heather's comeback also made her a YouTube sensation.

Get back up! (She did - and you can do the same.)

Now, as you know, many of the individuals profiled in this book are ordinary people, with extraordinary achievements. Heather isn't exactly an ordinary person; she's a state champion athlete who has also run in the Olympic trials. However, what happened to her – falling in a race – *is* very ordinary. We've all been there/done that, or we've seen it happen. (In fact, just last summer, I saw a young boy fall in a local 5K. He got up as well. Perhaps he saw Heather's video!)

Just as falling down can happen to all of us, we all have the potential to "*get back up*."

And the lesson, of course, applies beyond running. Most of us are too old (me) and too slow (me) to fight for a Big Ten championship, but each day we're faced with challenges and opportunities. The ability to "get back up" is usually the difference between success and failure, and although it theoretically should be easy, fear often gets in the way. The irony is that, for the most part, our fears are self-created. Psychologists like to say that *fear* stands for **F**antasized **E**xperiences **A**ppearing **R**eal.

There are examples of **FEAR** all around us.

- The FEAR of asking someone out...

- The FEAR of communicating with our children...
- The FEAR of going for a run or exercising...
- The FEAR of making prospecting calls...
- The FEAR of asking for a raise or promotion...

These FEARs, like most, are based upon the worry that something negative might happen. But do the negative responses we FEAR usually occur? Do our worries manifest? Not according to Mark Twain, who said, "I have lived a long life and had many troubles, most of which never happened!"

A few years ago, I was asked to help a sales professional named Lucy improve her success rate for gaining distribution of her products. I remember Lucy's manager telling me that she would invent every reason under the sun about why her customers wouldn't buy her new products: This customer won't like it because of the package. This customer doesn't buy this variety. This customer prefers the competitor. Most of her reasons were simply figments of her imagination.

Moreover, she was letting what happened *yesterday,* and her personal FEARs, dictate **unsupported** conclusions about why her customers wouldn't bite *today.* Her mind was running amok and because of these feelings, she was mired in a terrible "cold" streak.

"Get back up!" That's what I told her, but her FEARs had begun to paralyze her.

To make things feel more manageable, I suggested she temporarily scale back her goals in order to build some momentum. For the time being, and until she regained her confidence, I figured her best bet was to ask for less – to reduce the risk she FEARED her customers were perceiving. After all, what her mind was suggesting was that her customers found her proposals to be risky. Even though that was probably just an illusion, it made sense to set her sights just a bit lower. It's funny how that works. After a few successes, her momentum propelled her to heights far above where she was when her "perceived" trouble started.

I also suggested that she follow author Susan Jeffers' recommendation to "feel the fear and do it anyway." With a little coaxing, Lucy shifted her focus to today. She overcame emotional hurdles and put to use a wider range of sales tools: She got to know more people in her accounts, and she made a greater effort to know the customer's likes and dislikes. She looked for voids in her customer's selection and asked questions that forced her customers to think. She learned more about her own products, and her pre-call preparation soared to a whole new level. As a result, she gained a better understanding of her customer's goals, passions, and challenges.

Once she achieved some victories, her successes increased exponentially. She began to see herself as a successful, confident professional. She began learning from her failures in the same manner as she learned from her successes. It was far healthier than the fearful mindset that had thrown her for a loop.

She got back up.

Heather, the decorated champion, demonstrated this principle on the track, while Lucy did so in her professional life. My friend Mimi, on the other hand, has risen from unimaginable tragedy in her personal life to epitomize this key to success like no other.

Mimi likes to joke that she's won the "loss" Olympics. Surprisingly, that's as dark as her mood gets given that she's had more heartbreak in her life than anyone should ever be forced to endure.

In 2003, her daughter was born with a debilitating, life-shortening disease. Then the next year her son was diagnosed with leukemia. They both passed away in

2006. It was a terrible year for Mimi and her surviving 10-year-old son.

Mimi is known to say, "You don't know forever until you lose a child. When they take their last breath, you can't imagine how you're going to take another breath. You die with them, all the while thinking, 'How am I going to get through this?'"

But Mimi keeps breathing, for herself and for her son – a young man who has endured so much.

If you've studied self-improvement in any way, you've undoubtedly heard some variation of the expression – *It's not what happens to you in life, it's how you respond.*

Mimi responded to dark days by *getting back up* physically and emotionally.

She tells me that when you lose someone, anniversaries matter. 1 day, 1 month, 1 year.

Five years was a big one. Being a finely tuned endurance athlete, one of Mimi's aspirations was to do an Ironman triathlon to raise money for charity. The Ironman consists of a 2.4-mile swim, 112-mile bike ride and full marathon (26.2 miles). In a bit of meaningful irony, the Ironman race in Madison, Wisconsin was scheduled for September

11th, the day that marked the five-year anniversary of her son's passing.

So participating in that particular race became the goal. For Mimi, this was not about conquering this day of leisure (uh – misery), impressing others or checking it off the bucket list. She wanted to do this so she could tell her children, both here and *there…*

"Mommy's ok…"

She finished with a fine time that day, not that her time mattered. Perhaps she told herself she wouldn't have to run for 6 months, or ever again, if she found a way to taste the glory of the finish line. The truth is that she's "wicked determined" and her mentality is "strong like a rock!" (I'm signed up for her next "Mental Determination for Dummies" class…)

She didn't see herself as better than anyone else. In her view, many of her fellow competitors who were swimming, riding and running that day had stories to tell (including firefighter Rob, who completed the entire race in full uniform as a way of commemorating his fallen brothers from 9/11). So Mimi waited at the finish line and cheered in every last competitor.

Mimi not only challenged herself to compete in that grueling race on the five-year anniversary of her children's deaths, but also pushes herself to get back up each and every day after the losses she's endured. If she can *get back up* so can we!

That's just the way it works!

Chapter 8. Have a Plan

I didn't go there for a medal or for the thrill of victory. I simply wanted to run a local race with some friends. So one warm Sunday morning, we all toed the line at the Deerfield Dash 5K and 10K. It was a recreational crowd, to say the least. Lots people running with children and dogs, a guy wearing a full sweatsuit in the middle of summer, and a few runners carrying steaming cups of latte.

You get the picture. There weren't too many serious runners.

The race started and, after a few hundred yards, I realized that I was in first place - a position completely new to me. I came in second place once in a high school race (with more than two runners), but I never tasted victory.

Anyway, there I was, running right behind the police car. Could this be the day? Could I be destined for Deerfield Dash greatness? Was I going to be forever immortalized in the winner's circle – making me someone the locals would talk about for years to come? Would I be on the cover of the *Deerfield Review*? Would my finisher's photo be tweeted, re-tweeted and even given the exalted "favorite" status by running enthusiasts all over the world? Would I have something to post on my Facebook page besides what I ate for breakfast?

Have I built enough suspense? Ok, I'll get on with the story.

After another mile or so, the police car continued on the 10K route, while I followed the 5K route all by my lonesome. There were no other runners in sight. I was out in front, and that's when the trouble started.

I reached the proverbial fork in the road: a four-way intersection with no signs. I felt like Dorothy on the Yellow Brick Road, except I didn't have a scarecrow to tell me which way to go. Sadly, I don't think even The Wizard could have helped me that day.

And yes, you guessed it: I went the wrong way. When I reached the pivotal point, instead of going straight, I turned, despite there being nary a sign telling me to do so.

I'll tell you how the race ended at the end of this chapter. Suffice it to say, I wish I'd looked at a course map that morning, as that would've helped me know where to go. Undoubtedly, there would've have been a better outcome than almost ending up in a different area code.

Clearly, the day would have gone more smoothly if I'd *had a plan!*

You'll *outrun ordinary and achieve extraordinary* if you have a plan.

You'll have a much better chance of outrunning ordinary - if you have a plan

So my question to you is: Do you have a course map (a plan) for the busy race known as your day, or are you running ragged without a clue how to get to the finish line?

Here are a few suggestions for making each day as productive as possible:

Start the day with a brief planning session

One of the strongest pieces of advice I can give you is to start each day with a few quiet moments for planning. Too many individuals jump right to the first task on their mind, which isn't always the activity with the most importance. The planning session can be simple! While sipping your coffee, spend some time contemplating what would make this day successful. Think! Gauge your preparedness for the day. Anticipate (and handle proactively) anything that might knock you off your plan.

Here's another reason why it's important to spend a few minutes planning each morning. When you think of a customer, product or situation early on, your subconscious will kick into high gear and will work behind-the-scenes to generate solutions to your problems as you move through your day. Here's how to make this happen: Sit somewhere quietly with a legal pad. Write the name of an account or product or goal at the very top of the page. Then generate as many ideas related to that topic as possible and write every one of those thoughts down on your note pad. Capture *all* of your thoughts, including those that you might not initially think are helpful. By doing this, you'll engage a part of your brain called the *reticular activation system*. By stimulating your subconscious in this manner (essentially, giving your mind some material to work with), you'll get new ideas later on, when you least expect them.

Write out your daily objectives

Mental notes are vague and ill-defined. Writing your objectives pulls your energy to the target and helps ensure that you are sticking to your plan. It's always good to ask, "Is what I'm about to do more important than what I planned to do?" Ask this question anytime something unexpected threatens to change your course. At the same time, it's extraordinarily helpful to write down other things (e.g., new ideas, additional items for your to-do list) that pop into your head. Just this act alone not only clears your mind and allows for more creativity, but also increases the likelihood that you'll follow through.

Make sure to handle your priorities first thing in the morning, when you're at your best. It's easier to resist interruptions at this time and, if nothing else, when you address your most important items first, at least you will have accomplished these key concerns even if the day spirals out of control - which it probably will. Don't forget to review your notes, plans and objectives as the day goes on. Your situation (and your reality) is constantly changing. Plus, it's mentally nourishing to see what you've accomplished. It gives you a little boost as the day progresses.

Prepare for the defining moment

This may be a phrase that's new to you, so I'll define it. The defining moment is the point in time *when a roadblock, objection, or other obstacle presents itself.* It's also a period of time during which the critical ingredients of success are present. It's crucial, though, when this inevitable obstacle appears, that you react constructively in a manner that will move you closer to your goal. What most don't realize is that advance planning can help ensure a positive reaction to such events.

Spend some time anticipating roadblocks, objections and other obstacles and prepare a plan for handling these defining moments in a proactive manner. Often, these situations can be frustrating and result in delays or, worse, the inability to take action. The ironic part is that most of these frustrations are built upon negative self-talk and perceived scenarios that are usually just plain false. So as part of the planning process, take an objective look at what has happened in the past when you have faced challenges. Visualize the last time you encountered a frustrating situation. What happened? What thoughts were running through your mind? What did you do or not do? Consider what you could have done differently, and try to think of any positives associated with the situation.

Is it okay to allow for some negative time? Sure, you can vent about a difficulty, but only for a short time. If the mood drags on, your day will be forever altered. So take control of the situation. Make sure to ask, "What part of this challenge has my name on it?" Take 100% responsibility, as that will help you move forward.

Remember the "action" element of planning

The point I will make here is closely related to the above section on preparing for defining moments. However, I feel it's important enough (and overlooked enough) to warrant a separate section.

When you think of challenging situations that might arise and what your response to those will be, don't conduct that exercise only at the "30,000-foot view." Sure, you want to be cognizant of the big picture, but it's also crucial to drill down to specific actions. What, literally, will you *do* in a defining moment?

Let me illustrate with a story.

Before Memorial Day last year, our family stopped by the local ice cream store. The line was out the door, with just one lonely high school student serving customers.

Instead of helping her, the owner was off to the side refilling the gummi bear container. The line grew. And grew. I was standing there for 20 minutes, and I never saw the owner serve a single customer.

I decided to ask him a direct question: *"Think she needs some help?"*

I loved his response: *"Have to fill the candy. Can't sell the candy if there is no candy."*

I imagine the customers probably cared more about getting their ice cream before the holiday ended than being able to order a chewy object that many feel has no place in ice cream.

The owner had a challenging situation on his hands – massive numbers of customers expecting to be served in a short period of time. However, in responding to the situation, he failed to direct his actions to what was most important. Keeping a candy container filled might have been of some importance, but it was not **most important**.

So, when you plan and prepare, envision what you will *do* in any difficult situations you can foresee arising, in order to ensure that your actions are aligned with what's most important. You'll be able to have your ice cream and eat it, too.

Recap the day

Look at your calendar at the end of the day. Did the day go as planned? Was what happened what you wanted to happen? I'm sure a few fires popped up, but did you accomplish your most urgent and important tasks? Review and document whom you interacted with and whom you need to follow up with. Now is the time to start thinking about and noting what needs to happen for tomorrow to be a successful day. It's also enormously helpful to review the day's successes. According to sports psychologist Jim Fannin, "The last 30 minutes of every waking day are recorded and replayed that night by our subconscious minds 15 to 17 times more often than any other thought at any other time." Too often, the last thought before bed is what went wrong that day. Buck the trend and, at the very least, specify 3 good things that happened. Not only will you rest much easier, but you'll also wake up feeling like a champion, ready to *outrun ordinary and achieve extraordinary.*

So, as promised, here's how the Deerfield Dash ended! After a few minutes of running the wrong way, I got a sinking feeling that something was terribly amiss. I finally re-joined the course in time to come in 3rd place. I can't remember who won, but I do remember who came in 2nd place - a man pushing a twin baby jogger. Ouch! You'd think the diaper bag would have slowed him down…

Anyway, I wish I had looked at the course map. I wish I had prepared a plan because glory would have been mine.

And it can be yours as well. As long as you *have a plan!* As you look at your daily plan, please realize that you're not going to get everything done. The most successful people understand that. So they plan relentlessly to allocate, analyze, review and re-review their activities so they can be as efficient as possible.

In the end, these individuals still leave for the day with piles on their desks and most likely fall short of accomplishing everything they wanted to. But they get more done than the "just winging it" crowd.

That's just the way it works!

Chapter 9. Keep Going

Sometimes things don't go your way!

Not that I'm a poet at heart, but as I was writing this chapter, I was reminded of a famous poem. *To a Mouse* was written in 1786 by poet Robert Burns. In it, there's a great line that's stood the test of time:

The best laid schemes of mice and men, which is understood to mean that even the most carefully prepared plans may go wrong.

The athletes featured in this chapter know this all too well. One entered a competition which, despite his best efforts, didn't go as planned. In the heat of the battle he had to recalibrate his goals. The other had to overcome serious, often unexplained medical challenges that forced her to find a way to *keep going* forward, even when the outcome wouldn't be exactly what she had hoped for.

Alex Gold

Alex Gold is one of the most decorated runners in the history of Deerfield High School, a school with a loaded tradition of great cross country and track and field athletes. As it's the school my boys attend, I follow the team quite closely. In his high school career, Alex won too many races to name, but it's the race he ran at the 2013 state track meet that holds a special place in my heart and represents a great lesson for us all. I see that race as one of his best because of the decision he was forced to make in the midst of it – a decision that would define his last high school competition.

Being a huge fan of the sport, I was nervously watching the race on my laptop and cheering for Alex with every fiber of my being. For nearly half the race (four of the eight laps), he was in prime position near the head of the pack. The pace wasn't extremely fast, but many of these races are more tactical in nature. Nobody wants to go out too fast and be spent if the finish comes down to a sprint, which it usually does.

Near the end of the fourth lap, however, everything changed. Many of the pre-race favorites surged. Suddenly Alex was out of the picture - figuratively and literally. As I watched with concern, he was no longer anywhere on my computer screen. It was a staggering turn of events. I can only imagine how he felt.

I later learned that the leaders had run an extraordinarily fast lap. Alex tried to stay with them but couldn't. The truth is that he *also* picked up his pace but in spite of this had to re-calibrate his goals because the leaders were too far ahead. Winning the race was no longer a realistic goal.

And this re-calibration had to take place very quickly – maybe over the next 100 yards – because if he wasn't able to *dismiss the doubts* in his mind, negative thoughts could have wreaked all sort of havoc on his body and his performance.

The questions flew at him quickly. What would his new goal be? To earn all-state honors? To finish with a specific time, but one that was much slower than he had planned? To make his family and teammates proud?

Or would the disappointment and doubts take over…

His revamped goal was to earn all-state honors, and with this in mind, he *kept going.*

Alex kept going to keep regrets at bay, and for a multitude of other reasons. He kept going because it was his last meet in high school and he wanted to go out showing maximum effort. He kept going because his coach believed in him. He kept going because some of his future college teammates were competing and he wanted to show "what he was made of." Mostly though, he kept going because his teammates were there. His buddies, after driving almost five hours, were in the stands cheering his every step. Most of these boys still had high school eligibility remaining. In the future, they'd all find themselves in a similar situation – a day that wasn't *going to be their day* but a day when points and pride were still on the line. Alex felt a responsibility to all his supporters to keep going.

Alex missed all-state honors by one place in this race. Despite that disappointment, he was proud of the fact that he rebounded to finish with a great time, actually running his second mile faster than the first, which is a true sign of a strong attitude, a burning desire and a "won't give up/never say die" belief system! As he later reflected, "It often hurts to go for it, but it hurts even more to not go for it. You're never going to regret going for it but you have to keep going."

He went on to win a competitive national race against a truly elite field the following week – by a large margin! He credits his experience in the state meet as a factor that made his big victory possible.

Alex always hoped to win races, but for much of our next athlete's life, she'd have been pleased just to run around the block a few times.

Melissa Engel

I had a feeling that Melissa would be a tough runner because her dad, Rod, whom I met on my first day of cross country practice in 1980, was one of the toughest racers I ever faced. We both went out for the high school team and have been friends for most of our lives. I've been alongside (or, more accurately, slightly behind) Rod in some pretty challenging races, so I wasn't surprised to learn that Melissa, currently a pre-med student at Emory University, has *kept going* despite some severe physical challenges.

What I saw from this young lady on a frigidly cold Thanksgiving Day at the local "Turkey Trot" simply astounded me. Just a few weeks earlier, Melissa had been the innocent victim of some fraternity hijinks gone awry. While out running (a favorite pastime), she was struck on her ankle by an errantly thrown beer bottle. Although the bottle was empty, the force was strong enough to cause a deep cut and tendon damage and to land Melissa on crutches for several months.

While this is not a circumstance to be wished upon anybody, for it to have happened to Melissa seemed particularly cruel and unfair, since she had spent literally years of her life fighting through health issues to be able to run at all. But, true to form, Melissa fought once again and completed the entire Turkey Trot distance on her crutches!

Melissa has been battling physical challenges her entire life, some of which materially affected her high school running career. It wasn't enough that she was born with severe food allergies, making it dangerous for her to eat many staples that we all take for granted. Later, while in high school, Melissa was diagnosed with type 1 diabetes, a condition that requires constant vigilance.

Despite these setbacks, she "kept going." In preparation for her first cross country season, Melissa trained at a very high level, even doing hill repeats and speed workouts under the watchful eye of her pseudo-coach father! That year, she had an excellent sophomore cross country season, earning alternate status on the varsity squad.

Soon thereafter, she started feeling lethargic. This is how she explained the situation to me: "I wasn't feeling well. I felt tired all the time, almost as if I was running *underwater*."

The straw that broke the camel's back was the first outdoor track meet that spring where she fell apart during the race with a mile time about two minutes slower than her normal pace. The cause wasn't sore legs or overtraining, but a total lack of energy. She was devastated and humiliated to have done so poorly in a meet. Being an athlete with intense pride, Melissa grew increasingly frustrated by having to explain her symptoms to the coach, teammates and others. After all, it didn't look like anything was wrong with her, and Melissa feared that she would be labeled a hypochondriac.

She *ran* from doctor to doctor, all in an effort to run again. Her red blood cell count was dangerously low and a mystery to all the doctors who treated her. Iron infusions didn't help, nor did more advanced treatments. When we talked, she explained that her condition was the diametric opposite of the advantage athletes derive from blood-doping (which aims to increase the amount of oxygen in their red blood cells). She had less oxygen, which made it harder for her to breathe and excel at (or, on some days, even attempt) the activities she loved.

Despite the fact that there was no answer from the doctors, she kept going. There were good weeks and bad weeks. The best week before her senior year was a 2nd place finish out of 95 girls in her age group at the Rock 'n' Roll Chicago Half-Marathon.

Unfortunately, the bad weeks turned into bad months and wiped out her entire senior year. By then, all she was hoping to do was run for fitness and to feel good, not to compete.

Melissa's health eventually improved. Her blood counts have been excellent for some time now, and five miles at a brisk pace is no longer a challenge. She can beat her dad hands down; it's not even a contest! Her two-year (energy) funk is still a mystery, but as evidenced by the errant beer bottle, no matter what challenges she faces, Melissa finds a way to keep going.

The lesson for all of us from Alex and Melissa: Keep going. It might take longer than you expected. It might be more challenging than you expected, and the result may not be what you expected. It might require a course correction. You might have to adapt and change, but it's doable. Alex could have given up, and on that brutally cold Thanksgiving Day, Melissa had every right to stay in bed. However, people don't *outrun ordinary and achieve extraordinary* by hitting the snooze button!

That's just the way it works!

Chapter 10. Let It Slide

It's February 2014 as I write this chapter, and the Olympic Games are in full swing in Sochi, Russia.

During the games, my hometown paper *The Chicago Tribune* has been chronicling the fortunes of a local athlete named Katie Eberling. Eberling, a member of multiple world championship bobsled teams, was left off the final roster for Sochi.

This decision was described as very controversial.

Eberling was quoted in the paper as saying, "I'd be lying if I said it wasn't extremely hard and that I wasn't still trying to heal from it."

Nevertheless, she accompanied the team to Sochi and, instead of chasing her own dream, she spent her time helping others realize theirs. Reading about her selfless attitude and tireless support of her teammates, one can't help but agree with the newspaper's headline:

Her dream denied, she has to let it slide…

For this chapter, we'll be focusing on a success skill that all individuals desperately need in their toolkits: The ability, even when something seems grossly unfair, to *let it slide.*

As the *Tribune* reports, "Unlike most Olympic alternates, Eberling doesn't sit around waiting for a teammate to roll an ankle or come down with flu. She works. She spends hours at the track and in the workroom, helping to carry the squad's three massive sleds, sanding the blades to make them faster and taking training runs to give the three U.S. brakemen some rest and a scouting report at the bottom."

"Ultimately," the paper reports, "she feels that she is part of something bigger than herself," which to us laypeople is a refreshing attitude in an era of "ego driven" sports figures.

It's apparent that this athlete has the ability to put her needs aside for the good of others and to react with grace and dignity when things don't go exactly as planned. What makes her story so incredible to me is that the time frame for Olympic success seems short and possibly not so sweet. These athletes have physical body clocks that the rest of us probably can't even fathom. I'd gather that the expression "time flies" has more meaning for Olympic hopefuls than for the rest of us!

So in this context when something doesn't go as planned, the ability to let it slide must be extraordinarily difficult.

Do you have the ability to let water run off your back? To let it slide?

I know in high school there was a time when I acted in the exact opposite way. Our high school had a track meet every year called the Spartan Relays. It was our signature event and I desperately wanted to crack the lineup senior year. Unfortunately, I was left out of the meet in favor of some younger runners, who, in fairness, were probably faster than me.

I wore my hurt feelings front and center, and the following day, I walked off the team. Instead of "letting it slide" and supporting my teammates and a program that had given me so much, I reacted like a child. The reality is that if I had worked harder, the situation would have worked out in my favor. I was too young to understand the concept of "owning your result" and taking 100% responsibility for my actions! (We'll cover that topic in the next chapter!)

Anyway, the best of the best "let it slide" and live to fight another day.

This reminds me of Tom, a professional with whom I once worked. He demonstrated this success skill when he was passed over for the promotion he coveted. To make matters worse, his supervisor was less than forthcoming about the reasons why he wasn't selected. It was a dark time for Tom, as his choices were to either leave the company or stay in his current position for which he felt over-qualified.

I remember coaching Tom just after he got the disappointing news. This took place during the "great recession" when prospects for new employment were limited. More important, though, as Tom examined his life purpose, goals and passions, it became clear that he sincerely liked what he was doing. He actually enjoyed his job, his company and the industry. He felt that if he got to the root cause of being passed over for the promotion, there would be a good chance that things would work out for him down the line.

So he stayed, and his idea of "letting it slide" was finding out exactly what he needed to do to move forward. Many people would have stewed. Many would have given less effort. Some might have gone so far as to sabotage their employer by leaking secrets or bad-mouthing the company to customers and suppliers.

Not Tom! He went to work, both literally and figuratively. Not only did he bolster his efforts in the ordinary course of his job duties, but he also started asking the tough questions:

- Which specific skills should I improve to be considered for the next opening?
- What qualifications are you looking for?
- How will I be evaluated in the future?

He also engaged in some introspection:

- Am I portraying a positive attitude?
- Am I looking in the mirror to determine how I might improve?
- Am I taking 100% responsibility for my work and my performance?
- Am I learning enough about our products?
- Am I acting like a professional?
- Am I helping others?
- Am I *taking the road less traveled?*

That last question – *Am I taking the road less traveled?* – is vital. As Tom and I talked, I challenged him to truly assess the level of his commitment. Was he known as a "doer?" Was he known as a man of action? Was he making the necessary sacrifices?

Tom dug deeper and deeper. His questions weren't superficial; they were substantive and cut right to the bone. His attitude was that if he didn't seek feedback, the joke, ultimately, would be on him. Everyone except him would "be in the know" about his performance, and he'd end up being on the outside looking in. That scenario, he feared, could ultimately sabotage his career.

It turned out that the company's decision makers had confidence in Tom's ability to generate revenue and coach others in a one-to-one fashion. On the flip side, however, they questioned his ability to command a room. They worried about Tom's ability to garner the attention of his team and motivate professionals in a group setting. Apparently, when there were multiple people in attendance, Tom would look down and away and he'd often become anxious and somewhat unhinged.

Once Tom had an honest assessment of where to concentrate, the rest was simple. He and I worked on his skill set, together, and to further complement his efforts, he took a public speaking class at the local junior college. By the following year, he'd been promoted and was actively seeking even greater employment opportunities.

All of this happened because he took his situation in stride and let "the diss" slide.

And where's the Olympic bobsled hopeful headed in the future? With an attitude like that, the sky – not the top of the hill – is the limit.

That's just the way it works!

Chapter 11. Own Your Result

At one point in my life, every Tuesday morning started with a track workout.

I remember a certain Tuesday morning in particular. On this Tuesday, I dragged myself out of bed at 4:30 a.m., drove downtown to the health club, changed into running clothes and ran over to the track with my friends. It was a beautiful morning. Indian summer at its finest. I can remember the sun rising over Lake Michigan.

Back when I was training for marathons, most workouts were pretty intense, but this one took the cake. It was a total of 14 miles around the track at a fast pace. It felt like my best training session ever. My high school coach would've been so proud (if he could remember my name…)

"All Tuesday mornings should be like this," I thought to myself.

Back at the club and after my shower, I noticed people crowding around the TV. As I drove to work, I thought that seemed odd for a Tuesday morning. It wouldn't have caught my attention if it were afternoon; then it could have been people watching another riveting Cubs game, but that wouldn't have been the case in the morning.

My dad met me at the door of our family's business.

"A plane flew into the World Trade Center," he said, grimly. "I think the country is under attack."

We were just beginning to realize, and yet at the same time we had no way to fully comprehend, what was happening. We *did* know, however, that this would be no ordinary Tuesday morning.

We turned on the little TV in my office - the one that previously existed solely for the purpose of watching baseball games that the Cubs usually found a way to lose.

However, this was no game. Even if it had been, our team would be the losers because on that Tuesday morning, the world changed forever.

Many members of our team sat in my office in stunned silence. Someone (I can't remember who) was crying. Everyone was in a state of shock. Many people felt sick to their stomachs. Nobody felt like working. After a while, I started sending people home and closed the store for the day.

There would be no business this Tuesday morning.

However, as you know, Wednesday always follows Tuesday and no matter how terrible Tuesday is, you have to deal with the following day.

So on Wednesday morning, with heavy hearts and tons of uncertainty, we returned to work. Things were different.

There were questions.

Could our government protect us? Was our country going to be attacked again? Was air travel — one of the foundations of commerce in our country — safe? How long would it be before customers felt like shopping again?

We all had sinking feelings in the pits of our stomachs. What would we do Wednesday morning? In the end, despite incredible uncertainty, we focused our efforts on controlling what was within our control.

Own your result

In this chapter, I'll be sharing perhaps the most important element in your efforts to *outrun ordinary and achieve extraordinary*. The habit is called "own your result." Consider the following formula:

Event + Response = Outcome

Owning your result means your focal point in all cases is

your response to the events you experience. Though events over which you have no control may occur, you always have control over your response to such events. Moreover, any and all improvement in the way you respond will inevitably lead to better outcomes.

Owning your result means your thumbs are pointing at you, and not at someone else!

As we consider 9/11 all these years later, it's clear that our nation's collective goal after such a tragedy was not only to remember the victims, but also to make changes to ensure that a day like that would never happen again. The response was increased security on airplanes and at airports. The outcome: we all enjoy safer air travel. A fantastic outcome, even if it means removing our shoes once in a while.

In the case of our family business, we did all we could do the following day. We controlled what we could control. We took care of customers, we took care of our employees and we took care of each other. That was our best possible response to an event that shook us, and those around us, to our collective core. The best outcome we could hope for was a return to some sense of normalcy. So that's the atmosphere we worked so hard to create.

Do you take 100% responsibility for your actions - for your outcomes?

Jim Rohn, a famous speaker on human potential was known to say, "You can't pay someone to do your push-ups!" Such a simple quote that I interpret to mean, "Each and every one of us can achieve extraordinary, but WE have to do the work.

We all have the ability to *own our result*, no matter how challenging the situation.

Let's again use the dire events of 9/11 as an example. In the days that followed, we learned about the heroics of the passengers on United Airlines Flight 93. When the passengers, through conversations with loved ones, learned what was happening, they decided to take action. They tried to change the outcome.

The *event* was being trapped in an airplane that our enemies were using to bring America to its knees. The *response* was a quick plan and the simple words, "Let's roll!" With that, a group of passengers stormed the cockpit and tried to change their fate (the *outcome*). Tragically, the plane still crashed, but instead of coming down in our nation's capital, its final resting place was a field in rural Pennsylvania. Though terrible, this was actually a better outcome than our enemies wanted.

Even in the face of nearly 100% insurmountable odds and without a single weapon, these heroic passengers refused to take their fate sitting down. They tried valiantly to change the outcome. They paid the ultimate price, but in spite of being in the midst of such overwhelming danger, the passengers on Flight 93 still took the initiative to "own their result."

Thankfully most examples aren't so heavy. Often it's simple things in life. Want to lose weight? Eat less and exercise, and the outcomes are better health and a more pleasing result when you step on the scale. Want to be more prepared for your workday? Spend 15 minutes in the morning planning and thinking, and you'll find new and creative ways to achieve your goals. Don't feel that you have enough satisfying friendships? Socialize more frequently, open yourself up more often to others and develop a few interests outside of work. The result: more friends and more happiness.

Some people would rather *complain* than work on productive responses to their challenges. What's your strategy?

Author Jack Canfield suggests that the definition of complaining is *having a reference point of something I prefer but that I'm not willing to risk creating*. With a few simple questions and some honest reflection, it's easy to see that we can all take more responsibility in the important areas of our lives. It's not about keeping up with the next guy; it's about bettering ourselves each day. Moving the needle forward.

Ask yourself the following questions:

- If I were to take 5% more responsibility in my job duties, the following would happen...
- When I take shortcuts at work, the following occurs...
- In order to increase my self-esteem, I could...
- If I were to do one thing today to get closer to my

goals, I would…

- When I ignore things about myself that others know…

There's a famous thought that you've heard before in many variations. "It's not what happens to you, it's how you react to what happens to you." Does this resonate with you? I hope so. Taking 100% responsibility and "owning your result" is the first step.

If the people whose lives were most tragically affected by 9/11 can try to influence their outcomes, even in the context of unfathomable fear and danger, then imagine what you and I could do in our lives to *outrun ordinary and achieve extraordinary*.

There is no limit!

That's just the way it works!

Chapter 12. Pick Your Pack

Have you ever run a marathon? You know, the 26.2-mile distance that "strange" people run for fun on their day off from work. It's an arduous task to say the least and even harder if your hopes are pinned on running a certain time. Maintaining a particular pace can be especially difficult given all the distractions: the water stops, the people cheering, the other runners and, of course, the chafing (for which I recommend moisture-wicking fabrics and Vaseline).

Jokes aside, to sustain a certain speed I recommend **that you run with a pace group.**

Pace groups consist of runners with the same time goal. The leader of each group is a pacesetter - a trained runner who leads her group through the course at a certain pace. Typically, the leader has run many marathons, but in the role of pacesetter, her only goal is getting the group to the finish line at the prescribed pace.

Here's the rub of this chapter (and by rub I don't mean the type that's needed after the race).

If a runner picks his pack (i.e., joins a pace group), all he has to do is follow the blueprint laid out right in front of him. Just follow the person holding the 8:00 minutes per mile sign.

The great news is you can *pick your pack* in business and life, as well. If you want to achieve a higher level of success in any area of your life, seek out someone *who's already done what you want to do*. No matter what your goals are, it's likely that someone (somewhere) has had similar aspirations. *Their success leaves clues that can inspire and guide you!*

As I was writing this chapter, I conducted an ad-hoc experiment. I was working with a sales organization and was curious to know 1) if the younger professionals knew who the top producers were, and 2) if they had ever reached out to them for guidance.

I asked for a show of hands on the first question. Most people knew the go-to people; that much I suspected since the sales totals were posted on the walls in the sales room. It wasn't a "state secret." Next, I asked for a show of hands to determine who had reached out to the top three or four performers to talk shop.

If a pin had dropped, I would have heard it because there was nary a sound. If there was any sharing of ideas and strategies, nobody was willing to admit it!

Sadly, this response isn't limited to the company I was visiting. I find that many people resist the idea of seeking out the in-house expert, buying her a cup of coffee and having a chat to see what helpful advice or information might be shared.

Why? Well, there are many possible reasons:

1) It never occurs to them that they should seek that information…

2) It never occurs to them that others would supply that information…

3) It seems inconvenient and time-consuming…

4) It would mean change, and most people reckon they're just fine the way they are…

5) It means hard work, and most people don't want to work hard…

Do you see any of your thinking in the above reasons?

Pick your pack!

Ask for advice. Ask for feedback. Ask for guidance. Ask any of the following questions of someone who has done what you want to do:

- What draws you to this line of work? (This speaks to motivation and lets your mentor share something she will be, most likely, very proud to share.)

- What do you do outside of work to add to your success?
- As someone just starting out, where should I be concentrating my efforts?
- How do you "get back up" when you're having a bad day?
- Do you recommend any particular training programs, books, DVDs?
- Whom did you look to when you were in my position?
- What's a *must have* skill for my toolkit?
- What's another *must have* skill for my toolkit?
- What's yet another *must have* skill for my toolkit?
- Who's your inspiration and why?
- How do you get feedback on your performance?

By the way, when I was writing this chapter, I came up with the above list of questions in about five minutes. It's that easy and if you're stumped, simply look the individual you're speaking with in the eye and say, "Please tell me what needs to happen for me to achieve your level of success."

Take action. Just ask. (By the way, most people love helping. However, if Target A isn't interested, go to Target B. Don't worry about the rejection. If A says no, he or she wasn't helping you beforehand, so you're no worse off.)

Learn from those who can help you and distance yourself from those who might be holding you back. Spend time with the *pack* that's going places and extricate yourself from the grips of those stuck in quicksand because *you'll likely become like the people you spend the most time with.*

Think about it this way. Your mind is like a computer, a CPU (or central processing unit for short.) Attached to your mind is a keyboard. Everything you experience is input through this keyboard directly into your mind. EVERYTHING! Everything you see, everything you touch, everything you hear; it all goes into your mind.

If you read a book about self-esteem, that information is keyed into your CPU. If you attend a class to learn about the products in your industry, then that knowledge goes straight into the CPU. Unfortunately, the other side comes into play, as well. When you spend time with people having little or no work ethic, those traits go into the CPU. If you expose yourself to the Kardashians (not a fan), or any of the housewives who drink, scream and swear at each other all day long, that behavior makes an indelible imprint on your CPU.

Don't forget about your friends, either. Friends are one of the top sources of programs that get wired into your brain. Your brain records their words, their attitudes, and their feelings, just as easily as it records your own. This should make you question just how qualified a "programmer" each of your friends is and how much access they should have to your mental keyboard.

Outrunning ordinary and achieving extraordinary requires vigilance. Individuals who reach their potential don't let just anybody type on their keyboard. They guard their minds like a steel trap.

Yes, it's ok to have an outlet, a guilty pleasure of sorts – like chocolate or lavender bath salts. I know that work and life are challenging, to say the least. But if the unproductive (negative) people and experiences surrounding you outweigh the productive (positive) ones…

…*Then you're not picking your pack – the pack is picking ON you.*

Don't cede the keyboard. Pick your pack!

Just as novice and experienced runners alike rely on pace groups for success on race day, you should do the same. So ask for guidance and surround yourself with people who will help you finish your race in full stride. I won't see you at the finish line if you follow the pack that's heading the wrong way.

That's just the way it works!

Chapter 13. Rebound from Rejection

I remember the day like it was yesterday, though it was many years ago. It was during the fall of my freshman year of college, and on that day I was studying (mixed with napping) at a public library. I had recently transferred from the college I started out at to a different school closer to home, and I wasn't taking my academics very seriously. For some reason, while I was at the library that day, it dawned on me that the "fork in my academic road" was near. There were two paths: the first was a challenging road pointing toward a real sense of accomplishment, while the second was an easier "path of least resistance" leading in the direction of an outcome that I was less enthusiastic about.

I think I ultimately made the right choice about which path to follow, but it wasn't easy.

Let's back up a little. I was an underachiever in high school, and as I began applying to colleges during my senior year, I started getting my first real taste of rejection. Sure, there had been *some* rejection already (e.g., girls who made the wrong decision when I asked them out), but aside from that, it had been pretty smooth sailing.

Each day after school, seniors would race home to the mailbox looking for admissions letters. If a college wanted you, you'd receive a thick envelope containing not only your acceptance letter but also a big brochure and other materials. Conversely, if the news was "Go to college somewhere else," you'd receive a thin envelope.

I received a lot of thin envelopes.

I desperately wanted to attend Indiana University because that's where my entire world at that time was going. My best three friends in high school (Greg, John & Rod) and my twin sister Dana were all heading down to Bloomington, Indiana. Although I had a strong inkling of what the university's letter would say, it still stung when I opened the *thin* envelope they sent me. Reality was starting to settle in.

In the fall, I set off for the University of Iowa, an institution that had sent me a *thick* envelope, but also a school I never had any real desire to attend. I was unhappy from the start. I was living in temporary housing, and the people I felt closest to were hundreds of miles away – enjoying their college experience, together. I also missed my girlfriend/future wife, Jill, who was at home finishing high school. I felt lonely, and my mindset was not conducive to focusing on academics.

So a few weeks later, I left Iowa and returned home. The next day, I enrolled for the fall semester at DePaul University, but I still wasn't really thinking about getting my academic house in order. However, soon after that came the day on which I found myself sitting in the library thinking about the "fork in the road." And on that day, I did something that's an important element in any effort to *outrun ordinary and achieve extraordinary.* I made the decision to rebound from rejection – in this case, the rejection I had received from my college of choice.

Following my semester at DePaul, I spent a semester at Eastern Illinois University in Charleston, Illinois. Though it might have appeared to an outsider that I was "bouncing around," the truth is that I never lost sight of my overriding goal: To attend Indiana University the following fall. I was determined to *rebound from the rejection* I'd received from the school the year prior. Though overcoming that rejection would not be easy, I felt it would ultimately lead to greater happiness and fulfillment.

And that's precisely what happened. I really buckled down academically, which was difficult because I'd never done that before. However, the result of this effort was a year's worth of straight A's, and this strong upward trend in my grades resulted in a "yes" from Indiana University when I reapplied the following year.

That's the subject of this chapter. Overcoming rejection. In other chapters of this book, you've met (and will continue to meet) various individuals who have overcome a range of challenging circumstances. In this chapter, we'll discuss specifically how to move on and what to do when some person, club, organization or group of people tells you, "No!"

After all, every successful person in the world has heard a "no" at least once, and probably even a few times. It's how one responds that makes all the difference in the outcome.

Let's talk about some well-known people who have overcome "NO" in their lives and gone on to achieve great success.

We'll start with Albert Einstein. Though Einstein became widely known as a genius, he didn't always show such promise. Einstein didn't speak until he was four years old and didn't read until he was seven, causing his teachers and parents to think he was mentally handicapped, "slow" and anti-social. Eventually, according to various accounts of his life, he was expelled from school and was refused admittance to elite technical programs. He caught up pretty well in the end, winning a Nobel Prize and changing the face of modern physics.

There's also the example of my favorite hoops player, Michael Jordan (MJ), who led the Chicago Bulls to six NBA Championships in the 1990s but was cut from his high school basketball team. We all know how that story ended. Thank you for the memories, Michael!

Also consider Winston Churchill, the Nobel Prize-winning, twice-elected Prime Minster of the United Kingdom. He wasn't always as highly regarded as he is today. He struggled in school and failed sixth grade. It even took him three tries to pass the exam for the British Royal Military College. After school, he faced many years of political failures and was defeated in numerous elections for public office. He didn't become Prime Minister until he was well into his 60s. Now, we remember Churchill as one of the most influential figures of World War II.

Let's not forget author Jack Canfield. He tells everyone, to show the power of perseverance, that more than 140 publishers rejected his initial *Chicken Soup for the Soul* book. He's now sold 500 million books. That worked out well!

Last, but certainly not least, Ryne Sandberg, the Chicago Cubs' Hall-of-Fame second baseman heard "no" for a job he didn't even ask for. In 2011, when Theo Epstein took over as the Cubs' new President of Baseball Operations, he fired the current manager and publicly ruled out hiring the one manager (Sandberg) that most fans were clamoring for.

Sandberg, who was managing in the Philadelphia Phillies minor league system at the time, wasn't even asked to attend an interview because he didn't have any major league coaching experience. If Sandberg was upset by the perceived snub, he didn't show it. He continued to grind it out in the minor leagues and, after last season, was named the manager of the Phillies big league ball club. One could argue he made out much better in the long run. At least he doesn't have to see the Cubs lose nearly every day.

All of these famous individuals heard "no" from time to time just like you and I do.

I'd also like to share the stories of a couple individuals I know personally. My college roommate, Mark Schwartz (nicknamed "Schwa") has heard "no" many times, but that never stopped him from trying to achieve his goals. He's been a successful Certified Public Accountant (CPA) at an international accounting firm for many years; however, the early part of his career was riddled with starts, stops and rejection. Born and raised in Maryland, he matriculated at Indiana University with the goal of attending the school's highly acclaimed business program. Unfortunately, his grades weren't high enough to be accepted into the business school, so his dream of being a business major was dashed. His grades, in fact, were so low that he was at risk of being asked to leave school. Similar to me in my freshman year of college, Schwa came to his own "fork in the road." He buckled down, refocused his efforts and learned effective study habits. Ultimately, he raised his grades to a more acceptable level.

After college, his goal was to become a CPA. Talk about the ultimate "no" - it took him 10 tries to pass the CPA exam. 10 times! I have tremendous respect for him. He never gave up. He's *achieved extraordinary*, not because of the fact that he's well known for the type of work he does, but because he kept going in spite of so many "no's!"

My son Josh also heard "no" so many times that it nearly shattered a goal that was incredibly important to him. Here's what happened: On Josh's 16th birthday, he had two goals. First, to pass his driver's test. Second, to fly an aircraft solo for the first time. I guess it was akin to a badge of honor to accomplish both these feats on the day he turned 16. When I would ask why that timing was so important, he would reply, "Dad, you just don't understand!" It wasn't my first time hearing that!

Attaining his goal became a challenge because his instructor (sounding like a broken record) was constantly saying, "No, we can't fly" because of wind or rain or snow. (There is a saying that if you don't like the weather in Chicago, wait 15 minutes. Unfortunately, during this particular season, 15 minutes later it was *still* raining and/or snowing.) As Josh's birthday neared, he desperately needed the flight hours, but was continually rebuffed by high winds and inclement weather. That spring in question was Chicago's wettest and coldest in 60 years!

In spite of this, Josh never wavered. If one lesson was cancelled, instead of getting upset, he immediately scheduled the next one. It was a constant stream of "no" that spring, but Josh was undeterred, as he knew the end game was flying solo on his birthday. He accrued enough hours to achieve his goal just in the nick of time, and it was truly a sight to see! After getting his driver's license, he drove himself to the airport and calmly piloted a plane down the runway and up into the sky. He's been flying on cloud nine ever since.

So how did all these people come back from "no"? What can we learn from individuals who overcame rejection on a test, from a college admissions office or due to factors (like the weather) outside of their control?

Consider the following:

React with grace and dignity

When Ryne Sandberg was passed over for the Cubs job, he didn't throw a fit. He didn't go on a twitter rant or complain publicly about being *wronged.* Privately, he may have been stewing, and maybe he even used the snub for motivation, but his demeanor never wavered. He continued his work in the Phillies organization and was ultimately rewarded with their top job. And, as a result, he doesn't suffer the indignity of watching the Cubs every day. (Did I say that already?)

Learn something

Over time, my buddy Schwa learned what he needed to do to pass the CPA exam. He needed to learn how to be a student again. He needed to learn test-taking strategies. He needed to learn how to budget his time. He needed to understand what was expected on the exam, so he'd prepare for it in the right way.

A large part of my training practice is working with sales professionals who hear "no" all the time. Their natural tendency is often to respond by arguing with the customer or to think that, through shrewd handling of the objections, they can convince the customer to change her decision. Here's what I tell my sales pros: *You're not going to get the sale by changing your customer's mind; however, you might get the sale next time by sharing additional information (or benefits) that will help the customer change her own mind. For this to happen, the customer has to be the one doing the majority of the talking. You, on the other hand, should be listening and learning something that will increase your chances of success the next time.*

Take it personally, but not TOO personally

This is a tricky point so I'm going to choose my words carefully. Picture a sales professional leaving a sales call that didn't go very well. He's really down; the wound is fresh, and it hurts. Will he find a way to take the rejection personally, but not TOO personally?

Let's consider: Maybe this sales pro really screwed up. Perhaps he was unprepared both physically and mentally. If that's the case, then he needs to *look within himself* and make a few changes before the next call. In this situation, he should take the "no" personally.

But what if this sales pro was clicking on all cylinders and the buyer was simply having a bad day? What if the buyer's hands were truly tied? Maybe he wants to buy, but just not today; perhaps tomorrow would be a better day for him to say "yes." In this situation, taking a "no" too personally would be detrimental. I tell my professionals, "The customer is not saying 'no' to you, he or she is saying 'no' to your product or offer." But we have to be careful with this point. It's easy to say that every "no" gets you closer to a "yes," but that sentiment is only true if the sales pro uses the experience in some way to improve his ability to combine the right message with the right product.

When you receive a "no," look inward in order to assess whether you should make changes for the next try, but don't be lured into the trap of thinking it's *all* about you personally.

Drop the rope

Many sales professionals respond to "no" by continually banging their heads against the wall (trying the same or similar approach repeatedly, with mounting frustration). According to Aleesa Daley, a successful 10-year veteran of business software sales who consistently outperformed her quota, "Sometimes when desperate times call for desperate measures you have to *drop the rope.*"

Drop the rope is a tug-of-war reference. Sometimes, instead of pulling and pulling, you let go of the rope and approach the situation from an entirely new angle. She explained with an example: "I once had a prospect who was about to go with a lower-cost, decidedly inferior product which seemed out of character for an organization that had Apple computers on every desk. So I wished the client well (which you always have to do because you want to keep doors open), but asked them if they were going to get rid of all the Apple computers in their effort to save a few bucks. This started a discussion about the advantages and disadvantages of using the low-cost provider. I was prepared to respectfully go down fighting."

This creative way of re-framing the message was Aleesa's way of "dropping the rope" while taking a final stab at the business. It worked! Her prospect became a customer when the buyer realized that the disadvantage of using the low-cost provider was the risk that the company wouldn't provide a sufficiently high level of service. By resisting the urge to argue and cajole, Aleesa turned a "no" into a "yes" in a way that left her customer with a very positive impression.

Go to Plan B

When Josh was trying to accrue his required flight hours during the uncooperative weather, he learned that he had to have an alternative plan in case his initial one wasn't feasible. Josh started out by scheduling his flights on Saturdays. At first, if the rain caused one of his Saturdays to be cancelled, he wasn't able to reschedule for the next day because someone else would have already reserved the plane for Sunday.

Eventually, Josh developed his Plan B, which was to schedule the plane for both Saturday *and* Sunday of a given weekend. (This may seem obvious, but if you have teenagers, then you know getting them to stretch their thinking by even one day can be a challenge.) With his proactive strategy, if one day was washed out, he still had a chance of flying the next day. This is how he accumulated enough training hours to complete his birthday adventure.

Josh now knows what everyone should – that you won't *outrun ordinary and achieve extraordinary* without a back-up plan.

In conclusion (because this chapter should go "no" longer), I realize that nobody likes rejection. It's hurtful, disappointing and scary, especially if there are financial consequences. Think about it this way. History is filled with individuals who haven't accepted the answer "no." Sure, everybody hears the word, but over the long haul, individuals who *outrun ordinary and achieve extraordinary* have an "it's never over" attitude. You might not win NBA championships like Michael Jordan, but with this mindset you'll probably make the next sale (or whatever your goal might be)!

That's just the way it works!

Chapter 14. Role With It

Can one person make a difference in the lives of others?

Absolutely, and in this chapter, I'm going to introduce you to two amazing individuals. Both are courtesy of the academic world. Both are modest, yet are nevertheless amazing contributors to the community. Both understand that we all have the opportunity to *interpret our roles*.

Sure, all jobs have specific responsibilities. Imagine for a moment a housekeeper in a fancy Manhattan hotel. Her days consist of changing sheets and cleaning toilets, much of which can be pretty mindless work. Many of us would rather do anything in the world besides that. But once in a while, you encounter a housekeeper who seems like a ray of sunshine. She doesn't see her role as one of changing sheets and cleaning bathrooms; she sees what she does as much more than that. In her view, she is doing her part to ensure that her guests have everything they need for a wonderful stay, rather than defining her role narrowly as one who cleans up after others. It's her choice - a decision that she gets to make herself.

There are people all around us who have made the choice to elevate how they view their role in life. It's a choice that Coach Jeremy Kaufman and Tim Benton each made at some point. They could've looked at their roles, respectively, as coach and security guard, but they saw more. They wanted more, so they defined their positions as platforms to mold and enrich the lives of young people. Each day they *outrun ordinary and achieve extraordinary,* and the children in our community are far better off for their efforts.

Yes, one person can make a difference, provided he or she "roles with it."

Let's first introduce Coach Kaufman.

When my son Danny entered high school, he wanted to join a glamour sport . . . so he joined the cross country team. (Being a lifelong runner myself, I feel compelled to point out that football isn't the only glamour sport!)

As I listened to Coach Kaufman during the first parents' meeting, I came to a stark realization: The team's performance is important to him (and I'm sure he fancies a trip to the state championships every year), but that's not the limit to how he sees his role. He sees it as much more. He counts the following among his responsibilities: Building character. Helping young men make good choices and develop healthy habits. Urging teens to take accountability for their actions. Creating future leaders and encouraging the boys to do whatever it takes to realize their potential.

In short, Danny's coach sees his responsibility as that of a molder of young men. He believes in the boys and is always motivating them to reach higher. Always fostering teamwork and sharing ways for the team to go further. Encouraging the boys to see that every day is a great day. Always pointing out the connection between extra effort (and goal-setting) and success and continually stressing desire, family, dedication and what it means to be a champion.

Does he actually "reach" his runners with his higher-level development goals?

I believe so. I spoke with a few of his former runners. Here's what they had to say:

"We learned the importance of having goals and doing everything necessary to achieve them but, in the end, we learned from Coach that you get more enjoyment from knowing you did everything you could to reach a goal than from actually reaching it."

"He taught me that mental toughness leads to physical toughness - not the other way around. More than anything, he modeled for me how to be a decent, respectable man. He is for me the best role model I have, and I will always be grateful that he came into my life when he did."

"Before running for Coach, I wasn't very assertive at all. Coach taught me a raw sense of belief in myself that becomes self-fulfilling. When you let yourself see yourself achieving a goal, you start to believe in it and you'll do twice as much to accomplish it; especially with goals that take some nerve to envision accomplishing in the first place. I learned from Coach that it is okay to dream about those goals, and that has propelled me in academics, my social life, and as a musician."

I know that Coach Kaufman hears from his runners quite often. Recently he received a note from a former runner who is now in the military. The letter concluded with these words: *"I need to step out of my comfort zone and not take the easy road out. You taught me that, Coach!"*

Just as Danny's coach is making the most of his role to make a genuine difference, so is Tim Benton.

Tim is a security guard at my son's high school. He's like many school security guards in that he directs traffic, keeps teenagers safe and even escorts a few students to the dean's office every once in a while. But that's where the similarities end.

As part of his responsibilities, every morning (rain or shine) Tim stands in the high school parking lot directing traffic, and he does so with dramatic flair. I'll try to describe his repertoire. Remember Michael Jackson's moonwalk? I believe Tim has that move down cold. The performer Usher, an incredible dancer in his own right, could learn a thing from Tim, as well. Tim incorporates his "choreography" into his traffic-directing gestures, always with a smile and a wave to passing drivers. I wish you could see him!

At first, I didn't realize that many others were as inspired by Tim as I was. Whenever I'd drive my boys to school, I'd marvel at his disposition. So as I prepared to profile him in this book, I decided to get some video footage of Tim welcoming the students.

I posted the video to Facebook with a message of acknowledgment for Tim. The reaction was remarkable. By the end of the week, more than 1,000 people had "liked" the post and 150 people had shared the video. Most gratifying, though, were the more than 100 comments – all in admiration and appreciation for this man.

I was most astounded by the number of former students that chimed in. So it wasn't just me; the entire high school community (current and former students, as well as parents and administrators) values Tim - because of the way he conducts himself and lifts everyone's spirits. Tim likes to joke that his triglycerides shoot up over the holidays because of all the sweets and treats he gets from parents!

And why does he welcome everyone so emphatically each morning?

First, he wants to spread joy and happiness. As he explained to me, "I want the students and parents to know that school can be a good place – a happy place. Would it be *so* horrible if a teenager entered the building with a grin?"

Second, he realizes that he's often the first school employee that people in the community see each morning; he feels some responsibility to help people get their day started on the right foot.

Finally, he feels that if drivers are watching his actions, then they're, at the very least, paying attention - a big positive with all the moving buses, cars, pedestrians and, especially, student drivers in the vicinity!

Prior to his current role at the high school, Tim was a police officer for nearly 30 years. His "service" mindset was formed in part by a tragic event that occurred when he was applying to the police force.

One of the requirements for joining the force was passing a swimming test. Because he was a high school swimmer, Tim didn't fear this test; however, some of the applicants had never swum before. As he waited for his turn, Tim noticed a fellow applicant struggling to stay afloat. Fearing that the man was drowning, Tim jumped in the pool to try to help him, while most of the other applicants stood and watched. With the help of a swimming coach who was observing the test, he pulled the man out of the water and tried to save his life.

Sadly, the man didn't survive. However, Tim, in part due to his bravery, was chosen for the job.

This event in the water changed his outlook. Although he was always a giving soul, this incident shook him to the core. He pledged that from that point on, he would do everything in his power to bring honor (and service) to others through his actions. "A man had lost his life trying to get this job," Tim told me. "I wasn't going to take my responsibilities causally."

After retiring from the police force and spending time at home, Tim's wife Nancy suggested that he continue his work in the community – in part, to get out of the house each day! The high school was looking for a security guard, and before long Tim was hired.

There's more to Tim's game than fancy dance moves and hand signals. He's a learned guy, having studied Native American and Buddhist cultures (to name just a couple) for many years. He's guided by the premise that the warrior is impeccable and that *the warrior does his best at whatever he chooses to do.* To that end, Tim feels that if he has to stand outside to direct traffic, even in sub-zero temperatures, then he needs to do so to the best of his ability.

Tim also thinks a lot about the kids. Following Buddhist teachings, he strives to see their "suchness." To see who they are, individually, and what they're presenting. At age 62, many years separate him from the students, but he tries to see beyond their disguises - their tone and manner of dress. He feels that kids haven't changed over the years, as many would lead you to believe. He feels that *approachability* is the name of the game and a key for problem solving.

Tim knows that if the students feel comfortable enough to go talk to him, there's a smaller chance that problems will fester. He longs to be of service to the kids. Sure, he'll tell them to "get to class," but not before telling them how special they are.

I could continue singing Tim's praises, but I should probably bring this chapter to a close. Let me leave you with one final thought. My oldest son, Josh, loves Tim. Last spring, after Josh's high school graduation ceremony, I wanted desperately to take a family photo, but Josh was nowhere to be found. I discovered later that he was with Tim. He wanted a picture with Tim and a few last moments with a man who had treated him with such kindness. I suspected that they'd keep in touch and they have.

Tim and Coach Kaufman "role with it!" They're men who rise above their job titles and see their roles as much more, and our community is lucky to have them. You can "role with it" in your life, as well. If you're in sales, you can become a better partner to your customers. If you're a server in a restaurant, you can welcome your guests more genuinely. If you're a manager, you can continually mentor and lead instead of focusing solely on next week's goals. Only you can define how to view your role. The choice is yours!

That's just the way it works!

Chapter 15. Run Your Own Race

I should forewarn you. You may be reading the words of the next Beethoven…

One of my goals this year is to play the keyboard. I love listening to music. I love singing, too, although my voice has never been described as smooth and velvety. (My last glass of cabernet, maybe, but not my voice.)

I recently purchased a keyboard. My ultimate goal is to play a little ditty called "Love Song" (by a talented singer/songwriter named Sara Bareilles), but that may be a bit ambitious for right now.

So I started with a catchy, yet challenging, classic: "Mary Had a Little Lamb."

My 16-year-old son Danny also decided to try playing but chose a far more intricate song. While I was hunting and pecking at the keys in what seemed like slow motion, Danny was quickly kicking it into high gear. Before long, he had the first several verses of his song under control. I was still looking for "B flat."

Watching him get up to speed so much more quickly than I was, I felt disappointed (maybe even a bit disillusioned). My inner voice was having a field day

saying that I lacked the skills to make this keyboard
endeavor work.

By the way, we all have an inner voice, and that voice is
typically NOT whispering sweet nothings in our ears all
day long. Anytime we attempt to stretch, change, grow
or improve, the inner voice takes notice. The
comparisons begin to fly. Whether we're thinking about
running or sales or losing weight or playing the
keyboard, the inner voice pulls up a seat at the bar…

…And makes most people want to throw in the towel. I
know I wanted to, and it was only my first day learning
the keyboard.

Think about these lyrics from a Keith Urban song:

> *I'm drivin' way too fast*
> *And the interstate's jammed with*
> *Gunners like me afraid of coming in last*
> *But somewhere in the race we run*
> *We're coming undone…*

These words hit me right in the sweet spot. Learning to
play the keyboard wasn't a competition, and treating it as
one was causing me to "come undone."

It's natural to have thoughts comparing ourselves to
others; it's one's response to those thoughts that makes

all the difference in the world. I now realize that my keyboard endeavor isn't a race, and it doesn't matter if I come in last. How Danny plays is irrelevant to how I play. It just doesn't matter. What matters is that I practice persistence. (And get a lesson or two.)

So what do you do when your inner voice takes hold and raises doubts and comparisons?

Do you close up shop?

If your answer is yes, please don't be ashamed. We're all faced with ambitious goals and challenges that activate our inner voice. The reason is that there's a part of the brain (the amygdala) that resists change, so it throws everything and the kitchen sink at you – all in an effort to keep you stuck in your tracks.

Don't let the inner voice win. Fight back to fight forward.

Can everyone be great? Well, that's a difficult question. Beethoven probably possessed more piano acumen in his pinkie finger than I have in my entire body, but that's not the point. The point is that if I put my mind to a task and set reasonable goals, I can certainly be better than yesterday. I can be better next week than this week.

As Tom Connellan puts it in his book *The 1% Solution,* "You may not win all the time, but you can have a winner's heart if you do something better today than yesterday."

Ignore the inner voice and get started. Many people wait for the motivation to get started. And they wait and they wait and they wait. Because it's never really a good time to learn an instrument or lose 10 pounds or learn to speak French. The motivation never comes, and your body remains at rest.

Don't wait until you feel motivation to take action. Flip that premise 180 degrees and consider that instead of motivation leading to action, action can lead to motivation. Once you start something and feel some success, that great feeling will cause you to want more success. If your goal is to run a 5K race, resist being held back by 1) How fast your neighbor can cover that distance, or 2) the enormity of the distance. On day 1, lace up your shoes and force yourself to run around the block a few times. Do it again the next day and the following day. Follow American statesman and retired four-star General Colin Powell's guidance and "Do your best in the present."

Keep going and before you realize it, the wonderful feelings you're experiencing will motivate you to want more! Don't delay and don't worry about others.

It's only natural to desire Tom's success or Jane's physique or Phil's money. Many sales professionals I know compare themselves to others, despite the fact that they are not comparing "apples to apples." They all have different customers, sales routes, areas of expertise, levels of experience and skill sets.

Yet they compare nevertheless, and the comparisons simply aren't valid. Even seasoned professionals can end up thinking more about the other guy than their own individual business. Clearly, you can't start from where someone else is standing or where you feel they'll be next or where you'd like to be…

…You must start from where you are.

From Jack Canfield's book *The Success Principles*:

> Beginning in small, manageable steps gives you a great chance at long term success. Doing too much too fast not only overwhelms you, it can doom the effort to failure – thereby reinforcing the belief that it's difficult, if not impossible, to succeed. When you start with small, achievable steps that you can easily master, it reinforces your belief that you can easily improve!

As for me, now that I've mastered my first concerto ("Mary Had a Little Lamb"), I realize that it's not always a race. As long as you stay in the competition, then there's always a chance you'll finish. I'm moving on to "Jingle Bells" because Mary and her little lamb are safely in the rear-view mirror. I could play that tune blindfolded…

If I can begin learning a new skill and step outside my comfort zone, then you can do the same. Simply, identify an area of your life where you'd like to improve your skills, ignore what others are doing (or saying) and focus on small shifts in your own performance. Run your own race and you'll be making sweet music before you know it!

That's just the way it works!

Chapter 16. See the Finish Line

In 1997, my brother Brian valiantly completed his first Ironman triathlon in Vancouver. It was a thrilling day, as he covered approximately 140 miles by swimming, biking and running. What did I do for exercise that day? I ran 3 miles - slowly. It was a low point in my decline from a runner who entered (but didn't finish) a marathon every year to the coach potato I had become.

I didn't feel good about my sedentary lifestyle, and my brother's success spurred me to give a marathon one more shot. However, I knew that this time I had to wake up and smell the Gatorade.

I would have to change something about my approach to my races if I wanted to experience different results!

The day before my brother's Ironman race, I had been reading about how successful athletes visualize the courses they run, mountains they ski, etc. I came across a story (that I've seen repeated in numerous books and articles since) about an amazing Vietnam War veteran.

Major James Nesbeth spent seven years as a prisoner of war in North Vietnam. During those seven years, he was imprisoned in a cage that was approximately four and one-half feet high and five long. During almost the entire time he was imprisoned he saw no one, talked to no one and experienced no physical activity. In order to keep his sanity and his mind active, he used the art of visualization. Every day in his mind, he would play a game of golf. A full 18-hole game at his favorite course. In his mind, he would create the trees, the smell of the freshly trimmed grass, the wind, the songs of the birds. He created different weather conditions - windy spring days, overcast winter days and sunny summer mornings. He felt the grip of the club in his hands as he played his shots in his mind. The set-up, the down-swing and the follow-through on each shot. Watched the ball arc down the fairway and land at the exact spot he had selected. All in his mind. He did this seven days a week. Four hours a day. Eighteen holes. Seven years. When Major Nesbeth was finally released, he found that he had cut 20 strokes off his golfing average without having touched a golf club in seven years.

It was a compelling story, so with all this information in mind, I set out to make a few changes. I figured there was nothing to lose. If Major Nesbeth, during his years of captivity, had managed to improve his golf game immensely merely by visualizing, the least I could do was find a way to *see* myself crawling across the finish line!

See the finish line

No matter where you're trying to go in life, if your goal is to *outrun ordinary and achieve extraordinary*, visualization may just be one of the most important tools you have at your disposal. In short, visualization is the practice of seeing what you want so that you're more likely to get what you see.

When I first began my training, it was quite ugly but as the weight came off, my legs began moving somewhat faster. With trepidation and a hint of sweaty palms, I mailed in the race application but, even as I trained more frequently and saw my times improve, deep down I knew that something beyond this had to change. Getting off the couch was a significant first step, but if I prepared and executed as I had always done in the past, the outcome would be the same: NO FINISHER'S MEDAL!

Here's the change I made: The day before the marathon, I went to Grant Park in Chicago, the location of the finish line. I didn't go in work clothing or even training clothing. I went in race clothing: running hat, shades, my race t-shirt and racing shorts that were probably, in retrospect, a bit too short. I attached my race number to my singlet and I even wore a cheap medal from a local 5K race around my neck. That's how I planned to look the following day at the completion of the marathon.

Sometimes you just have to act "as if" you've already achieved your goal!

As my wife snapped photo after photo, I raised my arms in the air and let out a primal scream that might have awakened people living halfway around the world. Many other runners and race officials/volunteers in the vicinity stared at me. I can only imagine what they were thinking ... that pre-race jitters had gotten the best of me. Someone even asked if I was "ok," which at that point was debatable!

Not to date myself, but we took the film to the local one-hour photo. An hour later, I had a picture of me standing under the finish banner celebrating the accomplishment I wanted so desperately to achieve. As I carbo-loaded that evening with a plateful of pasta, I glanced at the photo. Before bed, I glanced at the photo. In the middle of the night, I glanced at the photo - and in the morning, as well. Right before the race began, I glanced at the photo. I saw the finish line.

With my eyes closed, I could see, hear and feel the finish line. I could see the last few yards and the stands filled with cheering spectators. I could see the clock and the banner overhead. I could hear the commotion and feel the asphalt under my feet. I could feel the weight of the finisher's medal around my neck.

As the race unfolded, my first revelation was that the doubt that had hampered me so often in previous attempts had taken the day off! Suddenly the middle miles (the part of the race where the excitement of the start has faded and you can't yet imagine the taste of the finish line) didn't loom so large. As the miles passed by, I realized, *"I'm getting closer to the finish line!"*

I passed the 14-mile mark.

I passed the 15-mile mark.

Then 20 miles were in the rear-view mirror!

Where was the WALL I had heard so much about? That point in every marathoner's journey where the body shuts down, usually around the 20-mile mark.

I never felt it! Instead, I was enjoying my race (and getting a kick out of all the signs, including the one that read, "I'd follow you, if I could keep up!" and another that shouted "SHUT UP LEGS!"). The visual I had internalized of finishing the race ended up blocking out all the negatives. Because the mind can only have one thought at a time, visions of cramps and abdominal distress were replaced by thoughts of the sound of adoring crowds and the visual of a large beverage after the race. (And the "beverage" I was *seeing was NOT* a glass of milk!)

22 miles down!

The 25-mile marker was a thing of beauty! I felt great, but for others it resembled the "walk of the living dead!" Runners were dropping like flies. Some were staggering, some were walking, and I even saw a few talking to themselves. Maybe they were promising their bodies they'd never, ever, run this distance again, if they could just make it one more mile.

I hit the final straightaway and never looked back. It wasn't like I was running on feathers, but it didn't feel like hot coals, either! When I crossed that finish line, I let out the primal scream of success that had escaped me in so many marathons past. I'd been saving that one up for a long time!

Seeing the finish line is what enabled me to finish the marathon that day, and the same visualization can work for you, regardless of the type of goal at hand.

Here's what happens when you visualize what you want:

Your subconscious mind reacts similarly to fantasy and reality. As long as your goal is reasonable, when you see that visual, your mind goes to work trying to make that image a reality. The main reason this occurs is that the gap between *what you have* and *what you want* is an uncomfortable feeling for your mind. It's called structural tension. To overcome this feeling, your mind goes to work to bridge the gap and make your vision a reality.

Here's an example of this principle in practice: I follow an author named Doug Bench, who studies and writes about the human mind. He recommends that when someone says, "How's it going?" you answer with a powerful and emotive word. He suggests that, for the sake of variety, you begin each day's response with a different letter of the alphabet (e.g., Monday – awesome, Tuesday – beautiful, Wednesday – charming, and so on). Bench reasons that when you throw the images associated with these adjectives out there, your subconscious has something to work towards. The reality of feeling "average" and the image of your day being "awesome" are inconsistent, so your mind will do whatever it takes to get you to "awesome!"

Let's dig deeper on this with my marathon story and the help of Jack Canfield's *Success Principles*. My reality, prior to that day in 1997, was that I had loads of trouble finishing marathons. I was always well trained, but my mind got in the way. When I finally conquered the demons that day, it was with the help of an image that showed me being **successful** at the marathon distance. The more I looked at the photo, the more my thinking improved.

First, my perception shifted. After visualizing success, I felt that I *could* complete the race. In the past, the doubt I created in my mind caused me to feel "heavy legs," which, in turn, sapped me of my will to finish the race. But that fall day in 1997 felt different. There was a sizable shift in my thinking. The image at the finish line helped me believe it was possible.

Second, my creativity increased. This shift was caused by the structural tension between my images and reality. In a race of this magnitude, being creative meant finding ways to take better care of my body. I stopped more frequently for water. I read more of the signs of support. I kept on eye on my nutrition. I ran a straight line and didn't weave, which cut down on the distance traveled, although that got harder to do as the race progressed!

Finally, my motivation to finish went through the roof. I knew what was possible and now I desperately wanted to taste the glory of the finish line. That feeling alone increased my motivation to heights I'd never experienced before.

See the finish line!

Whether your goals are related to life or to business, to your health or to your relationships, this key principle remains the same: The distance between your reality and your aspirations will lessen if you put the image of achievement in your mind.

If you want to lose weight, picture buying a new outfit in a smaller size. See the tag. Envision yourself trying the clothes on. Look in the mirror in the dressing room. You look good! Take a mental snapshot.

Similarly, if you want to make "the big sale," picture yourself closing the deal. See yourself shaking hands with the customer.

This avenue of thinking works, regardless of the nature of your goal.

You *will* get to the finish line (where I'll be waiting for you with a pat on the back or a banana … the choice is yours).

That's just the way it works!

Chapter 17. Stay on Course

If you're a recreational swimmer and have spent any time at the local pool, you know there's a straight blue line on the bottom. If you follow the blue line, then you should get to the other end relatively easily, without veering off course.

In open water swimming, unfortunately, no such line exists. Long ago, when I was a recreational triathlete, running and biking were my strengths, but swimming not so much. Most pieces of *driftwood* would give me a run for the money.

One year I did a triathlon in Central Florida called the "Intimidator." Entering a race with this name was my first mistake; I should have swum as fast as I could towards the "kiddie pool!" Anyway, as swimming was still a work in progress for me, after just a few minutes I was quite far behind the other swimmers. In addition, I was neglecting to apply what I knew about a technique called *tracking*. (When you *track*, you look up every few strokes to see where you're heading, which helps you continue in the right direction.) I soon found myself far off course in the choppy waters of Lake Clermont. I think I may have actually spotted the Gulf of Mexico!

The concept of tracking in open water swimming illustrates a valuable lesson about success and what it takes to *outrun ordinary and achieve extraordinary*. To achieve success and *stay on course* in your job, your career and your life, it pays to frequently be looking up (or tracking) to verify that you're going in the right direction and making the best moves.

If you take this lesson seriously, you'll gain the knowledge you need to move towards your goals. But you must be the type of individual who welcomes and is open to this information. Many people choose to go through life with a "blindfold" on, desperately trying to ignore the truth. Still others suffer from something behavioral scientists call dissonance.

You can't outrun ordinary and achieve extraordinary by going through life with a blindfold on!

Dissonance is a phenomenon whereby an individual perceives something about himself in a certain area of his professional or private life that's completely out of whack with what others think. For example, if I believe that everybody thinks I'm a swell dude, but most of my contemporaries would rather have multiple root canals than hang out with me, I'm suffering from dissonance. The ironic part in an example like this is that I'm the only one in the dark because as soon as I turn my back, everyone talks about me. The joke is, in effect, on me.

So, to make sure you're constantly moving towards your goals, make it a habit to solicit advice, help and suggestions from those around you.

For the purposes of this chapter, we'll concentrate on two easy ways to obtain feedback. The first approach is self-evaluation and the second is asking others what they think.

Self-evaluation

Do you remember "Snow White," the Disney fairy tale? In this story, the Queen is beautiful but also unspeakably wicked and vain. She possesses a magic mirror, which she asks every morning, "Magic mirror in my hand, who is the fairest in the land?" The mirror always replies, "My queen, you are the fairest in the land." The Queen is pleased with that because the magic mirror never lies.

But, eventually Snow White becomes even more beautiful than the Queen, and then when the Queen asks her mirror, it responds, "My queen, you are the fairest here so true. But Snow White is a thousand times more beautiful than you!"

Self-reflection and looking in the mirror is very helpful, but the mirror must be real. When you take a good, honest look and consider your thoughts critically, there's a much better chance for improvement. The fake mirror, on the other hand, leads to an overly inflated opinion of one's self. A positive self-image is, well, positive, but not if it runs amok!

So, take a deep breath, and look inside for answers to the following questions:

- Have I become complacent? (Am I accepting where I am, or am I still trying to improve? This is a high-priority question; 90% of the people I work with would benefit from contemplating this more!)
- Beyond the numbers, is my business up or down? (Maybe you're operating on all cylinders this year, but what do you see when you look out 24 months?)

- Is there anything I'm pretending not to know? (What keeps me up at night?)
- Is there anything I should be doing that I'm not currently doing? (This question scares the daylight out of most people – but it's a good one!)
- Am I enjoying what I do on a regular basis? (If not, what can you do to take greater pleasure in what you do?)
- Am I trying to be "all things to all people"? ("Serve people," but if you do too much, that's a recipe for disaster.)
- Am I giving it my all? (Am I taking *the road less traveled* and doing what others won't do?)
- Am I learning? (Reading, studying, listening, improving?)
- Am I moving forward? (Am I moving in the right direction? Am I any better at my job, life and relationships than last year at this time?)
- Do I feel good? Is there anything I'm consuming too much of, eating too much of, doing too much of? (Moderation is the name of the game.)

That last one hits home for me. In 2009, I quit drinking Diet Coke. As I looked in the *"real* mirror," I realized that drinking 12 cans (or more) a day for twenty-five years wasn't going to do me any favors down the road.

Remember to answer these questions truthfully. You're only fooling yourself if you're less than honest.

Ask for feedback from others

Feedback is called the *breakfast of champions* for a reason - because it's the nourishment that you need each day to *outrun ordinary*. Be willing to ask others for their feedback. Don't shy away from this information out of fear of what you might hear. The *truth* is the *truth*, and you're better off knowing it.

As Author Marshall Goldsmith sums up in his book, *What Got You Here Won't Get You There*:

- It's a whole lot easier to see our problems in others than it is to see the same problems within ourselves.
- Even though we may be able to deny our problems to ourselves, they may be very obvious to the people who are observing us.

So ask, but don't then immediately express your opinion. If you ask someone for feedback, you're setting the expectation that you'll listen and give his or her reply full consideration. Don't get mad at the messenger and don't give up on your goals, simply because corrective action is suggested. Look for patterns. If numerous people tell you that you never show any appreciation, take note. *Write a note* for that matter! Why resist or debate the issue? Unless you're on the debate team, would you rather have the success you desire or win a debate?

There are numerous ways to gain this feedback from others.

One way is to ask those closest to you to describe you with three adjectives. This is not an exercise for the faint of heart, but the results can be extraordinary. One variation of this exercise is to ask a friend/colleague to email some of your other friends, etc., asking for this information. By having someone other than yourself collect the responses, you'll be none the wiser as to who said what. Trying to figure that out is a waste of time anyway. Just go with it and use the information to your advantage!

You could also ask a few simple questions.

What am I doing well?

I love this question because it's not only inherently positive (and reinforces which behaviors to continue), but it also will give you an indication of how closely the things you do well are correlated with what others feel are important. For example, if YOU feel that your greatest strength is sharing product information with customers, but by asking this question, you learn that they are more interested in merchandising ideas, you may be wasting your time with all the glossy brochures. That's good to know!

What could I do better?

This is another simple, effective question, but here's a quick word to the wise. Often, as if conditioned by Pavlov, when you asked questions like this, your colleagues, friends, family, customers or clients will say, "Everything is great!" (This is especially true if you don't often ask these types of questions.) Push back, gently, on vague answers. If a client says, "Everything is great!" say, "Thank you! If there is one thing I should work on, what would that be?"

One more note on obtaining feedback. Ask in whatever manner makes you most comfortable. Just ask. Also, any of the questions I suggested you ask yourself in the mirror are perfect ways to ask for feedback from others. Just change the wording a bit. Change "Am I trying to be all things to all people?" to "On a scale of 1 to 10, how well do I balance the need to please others with the need achieve my goals in a efficient and productive manner?"

When the feedback stings

Even when you don't like what you hear, listen and take note. Give yourself a pat on the back for asking. That's more than most do. Say "thank you" with a smile, not a grimace. Responding to feedback with explanations and justifications is a massive waste of time. That sort of bellyaching in response to unpleasant feedback will make it a near certainty that those closest to you will hesitate before sharing their honest feedback with you ever again. Instead of hosting a "pity party," re-focus your efforts to improve in the areas identified. Remember that you can't *stay on course* and run your life to your fullest potential without asking the tough questions.

That's just the way it works!

Chapter 18. Stretch

When I was in high school, I saw an image in *Runner's World* magazine that affected me deeply – a sign that read: *If there's such a thing as a runner's hallowed ground, you're standing on it.*

The sign was from the start of the Boston Marathon. The "hallowed ground" mentioned was located in Hopkinton, Massachusetts, precisely 26.2 miles from the finish of arguably the world's greatest marathon.

Simply put, I felt I had to get there, and the pursuit of *Boston* became my goal! I wanted so desperately to get there because I had something to prove. Back in high school, I was an *average* runner, but I always believed I could be better than that. As I reflect upon those days, I realize that I took many races off. I could count on one hand the number of races in which I gave my all, and I wanted to rectify that by qualifying for and running Boston. Given my historical pace, I felt that the qualifying time was a *stretch* - a goal that I would have to work extremely hard to accomplish.

It took me longer than I hoped to get the opportunity to run up Boston's famous "Heartbreak Hill," but I eventually achieved my goal. It was a priceless experience and my hope is that, with the help of the lessons in this book, you, too, will have the tools to achieve your most ambitious goals. The experiences of the people profiled in this chapter are instructive with respect to the first step in your journey: articulating your "stretch" goals.

Lionel and Daniela Garcia

These avid runners and dog lovers set and achieved an ambitious goal (a stretch goal) after getting engaged on Christmas Eve in 2012. They planned to get married in Disney World on January 8, 2014 and then spend the next four days competing in a uniquely physically demanding event called *The Dopey Challenge* – all the while raising money for charities that help animals, a cause Lionel and Daniela both care deeply about.

For those of you unfamiliar with *The Dopey Challenge,* this form of self-torture consists of a 3.1-mile run on Thursday, a 6.2-mile run on Friday and a half-marathon (13.1 miles) on Saturday. As if that's not enough, Sunday is the main event – a full marathon with thousands of runners who have been resting, not running, the prior three days! The combination of these races poses a daunting endurance challenge, even for the most physically fit participants.

One doesn't *outrun ordinary and achieve extraordinary* without *stretch* goals. Andrew Carnegie, thought to be

The far target will command your thoughts, liberate your energy, and inspire your hopes

the richest man in the early 1900s said, "If you want to be happy, set a goal that commands your thoughts, liberates your energy, and inspires your hopes." Most of the goals we set for ourselves focus on improving our life in the moment. Making the next mortgage payment on time, losing 5 pounds or asking for a raise at work. Stretch goals do more than that. These goals represent higher-level aspirations that are worth pursuing with passion and that will give you something to focus on a little bit each day until they're reached.

That's what *The Dopey Challenge* did for Lionel and Daniela. Before the big day, they faced numerous challenges. A big move, a burglary, a serious injury to their beloved dog, Phoebe, and weather delays galore. They arrived in Florida at 3 a.m. the morning of their wedding. Any of these obstacles could have understandably derailed the pair's plans, but the "stretch" of their goal helped them keep their focus. As Daniela describes her thinking 24 miles into the last leg of their arduous journey, "I didn't think I was going to finish but I didn't come this far (to quit). So at that point I set a mini-goal, and told my body we wouldn't run for two days after we crossed the finish line. It worked!"

Lionel and Daniela accomplished their stretch goal of creating a wedding experience that was unique, creative and memorable. Lionel shared that the more they talked about it and realized how crazy the idea sounded…the more excited they were to do it! That's the whole idea. When the stretch goal becomes emotive, it's more likely that you'll do what it takes to see it through.

Miriam Laundry

Miriam has an extraordinary stretch goal. She's trying to set the Guinness World Record for the largest online book discussion. Her inspiration is both tragic and empowering.

As Miriam puts it:

> It is in the times of our biggest despairs that we find our purpose. This journey started for me on

June 9th, 2012. On this day, I was at the hospital waiting to go home with my 2-day-old baby, when I heard the news that would change everything for me. My husband told me that our 17-year-old niece had taken her life. This was a complete shock! The days and weeks that followed are a complete blur. Between caring for a new baby and the sadness of our loss, I don't remember very much of that summer.

Miriam's husband noticed that she wasn't herself so he suggested that she attend a week-long transformational program. Miriam tells me, "From that experience, I came back a new person, a person with a purpose. It was there that I figured out what I was meant to do." She took an intensive writing course and began writing. At first, her plan was to write a book for adults, but she quickly shifted her focus to writing a children's book because she kept thinking that she needed to do something to help children grow to be happy and confident. Children became her audience and now the goal of teaching children a positive, empowering message occupies her thoughts.

Miriam wants to help kids believe that they can overcome any difficult situation, and writing is her way of doing something constructive to help them grow into empowered teenagers and adults.

The "stretch" part of her goal is to become a part of history by having record numbers of people commit to reading her children's book *I CAN Believe in Myself* and commenting online as a means of engaging children, classrooms and families in the discussion around self-confidence and mental health!

Miriam's goal is to inspire others…and others have taken note. She recently was honored with a Winspiration Award. Since 2003, Winspiration Awards have been presented 11 times on the occasion of Winspiration Day. The award recognizes exceptional and inspiring individuals for impressive civic engagement. This award is a meaningful symbol of recognition for Miriam as she continues to pursue her stretch goal of having a broad impact on children's self-esteem.

Christian Bucks

While writing this chapter, I stumbled upon an incredible story of a 2nd grader "stretching" to help his fellow classmates. The following is from the *Huffington Post* website.

Second-grader Christian Bucks, of York, Pennsylvania, knew that some of his classmates felt lonely during recess, and he decided to do something about it. His simple, utterly heartwarming solution was to install a playground 'buddy bench.' As reported by the *York Daily Record*, a buddy bench is a designated seating area where students feeling lonely or upset can seek camaraderie.

After learning of a school in Germany with a "buddy bench," Christian pitched the idea to his principal, who immediately got on board. Christian told the *Record* that he hopes the bench will help "grow our dream circle of friends."

We could learn a lot from this young man, who is "stretching" to make sure all students have someone to play with. Talk about achieving extraordinary!

Creating your "stretch goal"

Ready to start creating a meaningful stretch goal? First, let's talk a bit about goal setting, in general. Michael Hyatt, author of *Platform: Get Noticed in a Noisy World,* is an expert on the subject.

He suggests the following 5 guidelines be followed when setting goals of any type:

1) Focus on no more than 5-7 goals. Productivity studies have shown that most people can only effectively concentrate on this number of things at a time.

2) Set "SMART" goals, defined as goals that meet the following five criteria: Specific, Measurable, Actionable, Realistic and Timely. I will expand a bit further on this point by giving a few examples. Saying "I'll write one chapter each week" is more specific, measurable, and action-oriented than simply saying "I'll write more often." To incorporate the element of timing into the articulation of the goal, one could say "I'll write one chapter each week for the next ten weeks, and I'll turn these chapters in to my publisher by 5 p.m. Central Standard Time each Friday afternoon." (Keep in mind that many experts suggest specifying timing down to a precise hour.) Finally, it's important to make sure that your goals, even the most challenging ones, are realistic so that you don't get overwhelmed to the point of inaction.

3) Write your goals down to "formally" state your intention and set things in motion. (You'll read more on this in the next section.)

4) Keep your goals front and center by reviewing them frequently and asking yourself, "What's the next step I need to take to move toward this goal?"

5) Share your goals with people who believe in you. Forget the naysayers. I couldn't agree more! There's no sense in inviting anyone into your inner circle if they're going to burst your bubble. (Circle, bubble: there's a creative expression in there somewhere…I'll let you know when I figure it out!)

Silliness aside, the reality is that there are so many great resources on goal setting, so *after* you've read this book, stop by a bookstore or browse the Internet for more information on this topic!

Now, back to our discussion of "stretch" goals, specifically. When working toward these most ambitious goals, it's helpful to incorporate some additional action items. There's a simple formula I follow from Jack Canfield, co-author of the *Chicken Soup for the Soul* book series. The formula consists of three steps, and I'll illustrate each with a personal story.

Step 1: Write your breakthrough goal down.

A stretch goal, an aspiration of great magnitude, is something that will propel you much further ahead in business, sports, relationships, or just about any facet of life than you would've gotten without it. The example that Jack uses to highlight the difference between a regular goal and a stretch goal is from the world of football. Running the ball for a four-yard gain is nice, but a 50-yard bomb gets you closer to the end zone much more quickly.

Many years ago, my stretch goal was to be accepted into Northwestern University's Kellogg School of Management. This was a stretch for me because I was an underachiever in high school. I was in the half of the class that made the upper half possible…and I didn't take academics seriously until college. When I decided to take the plunge and throw the 50-yard bomb, I wanted to go to Northwestern, one of the best MBA programs in the country. The challenge was that a school of this caliber accepted the brightest young business minds in the country and I wasn't sure I had the grades, the scores or the intellect to be included in such a group.

But I wanted it (and I believed it to be realistic, though challenging), so I articulated the goal and wrote it down.

I will begin work on my MBA at Northwestern in the fall quarter of 1994.

Putting pen to paper was an important first step. There is extensive research showing that documenting your goals increases your chances of reaching them by a wide margin. In fact, *USA Today* reported that writing down your goals increases the probability of success by 1100%. The paper further said that only 4% of all people who don't take this step actually reach their objectives. There's even more compelling evidence from noted Professor David Kohl of Virginia Tech, who says, "People who write down their goals earn 9 times as much over their lifetimes as people who don't!"

Step 2: Visualize how your life would change as a result of accomplishing this goal. What would you be doing, seeing and feeling?

Many students in MBA programs seek a new job, valued promotion or career change. My story was different. At that time, I was working my way up in our family's business, but I felt my life would change for the better with this degree. I'd be more confident, more knowledgeable about my job responsibilities and more marketable if I eventually sold the business - which I ultimately did.

I visualized the success I'd have as a result of my additional knowledge. I visualized the amazing people that I'd meet in the program. I visualized the diploma hanging in my office, and I visualized the group interaction and the chance to learn from such a talented group of peers.

I visualized what it would be like to attend class at Northwestern. What it would be like to buy my books – and, of course, a purple Wildcat hat. I suffered through the football games as if I were already a student. I visited the school at different times of day as if I belonged there. I walked through the door of a classroom pretending I was on time for class. I asked the admissions office if I could audit a class, or sit in on a class one evening while I was still in the process of applying.

This last part, actually sitting in the classroom, helped immensely with my goal setting. To give your subconscious the clearest possible visual, it's best to have a firsthand account. In other words, peering through the window while a lecture is taking place doesn't send as strong an image as sitting in the fourth row of a packed auditorium. Feeling the presence of the other students. Hearing the professor's words. Noticing if the room is hot or cold, loud or quiet.

As you'll understand from reading the chapter on visualization ("See the Finish Line"), forming a detailed mental image in this way created structural tension in my mind, causing my subconscious to work to bridge the gap between my current situation and my goal of earning my MBA from Northwestern.

Step 3: Now write down an affirmation for your breakthrough goal.

As I contemplated the admissions process, I knew a key element of my success would be achieving a high score on the Graduate Management Admissions Test (GMAT). My college grades and work experience were set and I knew, based upon my admissions interview, that a high GMAT score would virtually ensure my acceptance into the program. To "psych myself up," I repeated a simple mantra:

I am confidently and spectacularly scoring 600 points or higher on the GMAT exam.

The mantra included the words "confidently and spectacularly" because these emotive words made the affirmation stronger. It's important to attach an emotion because when you do, the words have a greater effect on your mind. I also specified "600 points or higher" because there was no reason to limit myself. If I was going to put in the effort, I wanted my mind to see the highest achievement possible.

Every morning while preparing for work and on the weekend before heading out to study at the library, I repeated those words out loud. I repeated that mantra while sitting in my office (when nobody was around, of course) and while driving in my car. My goal was to verbalize it at least three times a day to get it "set" into my subconscious. As a result, my confidence and determination soared.

My conscious thinking, which admittedly had been pessimistic at first, began to shift. I started to believe that earning a high score and attending Northwestern were possible. I became more creative and found more time to study, despite working more than 60 hours a week.

I missed my GMAT test goal by 10 points, but the score was strong enough for me to reach my stretch goal. I was accepted into the program!

I'd like to make one last, very important point regarding goals. What if I had missed my target GMAT score by 30 points? What if Miriam falls short in her attempt to earn Guinness Book of World Record distinction and only achieves (gasp!) the 2nd most attended online book discussion? Is that failure? Should her effort to build self-esteem in children be deemed a waste?

The answer, of course, is a resounding "NO!" As you evaluate the success of your endeavors, it's imperative that you assess the situation from 30,000 feet. If Miriam's message about the importance of self-esteem in children reaches 14,000 families (instead of 15,000), the effort is still an undeniable success. She'd be wise, in that case, to focus her thoughts on the number of people she reached, instead of the number she didn't reach.

So be proud of what you achieve and don't be afraid to "stretch." Set the bar high because life is not a limbo contest!

Lionel, Daniela, Miriam and Christian are all examples of individuals who succeeded in setting the bar high and "stretching" for it. They're *outrunning ordinary and achieving extraordinary.* To join them - write your goal down, visualize what reaching it will mean to you and create an affirmation to lock it into your subconscious. They're all going places and you can do the same.

That's just the way it works!

Chapter 19. Take the Road Less Traveled

You know those models that grace the covers of fitness magazines? I recently had the opportunity to meet one, and the great news is she talked to me!

It got me wondering…

Are cover models born with perfect bodies and charmed lives? Did they come into this world with exquisitely toned six-packs while many other folks (including me) have what would be more aptly described as mini-kegs?

Allow me to go out on a limb on this topic. I imagine that while it's quite challenging to be in that kind of shape all the time, many cover models probably started out with fit and trim bodies. However, that was not the case with the person I met, fitness model Lori Harder.

Lori was overweight as a child and hailed from a family of non-exercisers. As a result, she suffered and missed the chance to partake in activities such as dance and gymnastics, which she desperately wanted to enjoy. In her words, *"I really struggled in school and was made fun of daily for my weight. As a result, I ended up being home schooled throughout high school."*

Lori shared how hard it was growing up this way. Eventually, as a teen, she made the decision to change and asked her mom to buy fitness magazines. She ripped out the photos and plastered the images of fit people all over her bedroom walls. She wanted to become one of them. Slowly the transformation began and the baby fat was replaced with muscle.

In the process, Lori was outrunning ordinary and becoming extraordinary.

As time went on, she began to envision the possibility of being on the cover of a fitness magazine, not just for the sake of setting a personal goal, but more importantly to show other women what could be done with a strong focus on health and wellness. To achieve that goal, Lori knew she'd have to persevere - not only physically with her product (her body and mind), but also with the way she marketed herself and her company. She'd have to stay strong and press ahead even when being told that she "wasn't the right look" or didn't fit the "girl next door" image. And while waiting for the big break, she'd have to **take the road less traveled** instead of the easy way out.

That's the principle we'll focus on in this chapter: Doing what others won't do. Taking the actions others won't take and, most importantly, making the sacrifices that others won't make.

Taking the road less traveled.

There's a reason why the road less traveled has less traffic. It's because most people choose a path that requires making fewer sacrifices.

Because I'd never met someone like Lori before, it never occurred to me what an individual like this needs to do each day to stay fit and remain *cover-worthy.*

Lori shared that her sacrifices often include the following:

- Avoiding late nights
- Keeping sweets at bay
- Skipping carbohydrates
- Abstaining from drinking alcohol
- Missing out on some of the good times

Now, it's not that she doesn't live life to the fullest. She actually enjoys working out and running on the beach. She genuinely likes eating healthy foods. Once in a while she even folds like a lawn chair and eats a few slices of pizza. Certainly, she's not leaving *every* party at 9 p.m. to get enough beauty sleep.

Recently, Lori was featured in *Strong Magazine.* The following paragraph from her cover article suggests that fitness doesn't equal deprivation:

> We really question ourselves thanks to so many food fads out there. I used to think carbs were bad and desserts during the week were forbidden, which led me down the path of binging and feeling massive guilt and fears towards food. Now I truly enjoy a very balanced meal plan all week long. I don't deprive myself and I have a little bit of chocolate every day. I also love my glass or two of red wine on the weekend.

But the key with her is she resists the temptations more than the rest of us do, and she gives maximum effort.

Do you always give maximum effort? If you don't – what's the reason? For example, just today I ran five miles on the treadmill. It's better than nothing, but I could have done more. Frankly, I was more interested in where to have lunch. In retrospect, I could have sculpted my abs a bit. Not that this is necessarily my goal, but there's a reason why *Men's Health* isn't burning up my mobile number. It's because I don't make those sacrifices.

Lori's effort and sacrifices are why she's on the cover of a magazine. She wasn't born cover-ready.

Are you taking the necessary steps to reach your potential? Are you taking the road less traveled? Are you making the sacrifices that will catapult your career forward? Are you taking action? Most importantly, are you willing to pay the price that most won't pay?

Jack Canfield knows a thing or two about success, having authored more than 100 books on successful people. In *The Success Principles* he says:

> Though many things are typically required to reach a successful outcome, the *willingness* to do what's required adds that extra dimension to the mix that helps you persevere in the face of overwhelming challenges, setbacks, pain and even personal injury.

Ask yourself: What am I *willing* to give up to achieve my goals?

Also carefully consider the following questions: What am I pretending not to know about my current situation? And how is the answer to that preventing me from reaching my goals?

I posed these questions to Frank, a professional whom I coached recently. His sales numbers were sagging and his performance, which had previously been strong, was suddenly flagging. After a few conversations, he admitted that he had eliminated one critical aspect of his daily planning. He was skipping the nightly review of the next day's objectives, a step that had once helped him be so well prepared. He was pretending not to notice that his effort had slipped in this area and he was blaming the slide on the weather and other external factors.

Where once he was taking the *road less traveled* by putting in the extra effort, he was now actively looking for shortcuts.

Similarly, I talked to a manager who was pretending not to notice that the relationships he once enjoyed with his team members were deteriorating. When times were good, the manager spent a fair amount of time coaching his people individually. This action allowed him to keep closer tabs on their successes, compliment them and provide on-the-spot guidance quickly and efficiently in order to maintain a high level of credibility with the team.

Once the manager began to spend less time coaching, the focus became negativity. He simply wasn't *present* enough to see the good stuff, so the conversations inevitably shifted to missed goals, etc.

The action he wasn't taking was scheduling coaching calls. He was pretending that other work was more important than building and maintaining his team's morale. He was pretending not to notice the warning signs.

Most of us are pretending not to know something. The pants are getting a smidge tighter. The alcohol flows a bit more freely. We're spending too many mornings under the covers, instead of on the treadmill.

Here's an exercise to drive the point home. Sit face to face with someone you feel comfortable with. The person with the shortest hair goes first. (I like this method because I typically have the shortest hair in the room!)

This person asks the other: *"What are you pretending not to notice?"* Ask and answer this back and forth. After a while, something constructive will emerge. Since both parties have to share, that should help each individual be more comfortable going to a potentially vulnerable-feeling place. Afterwards, talk about what you each can do to address "what you're pretending not to notice."

We began this chapter talking about models, so model the best behavior and be vulnerable. You won't outrun ordinary by hiding under the covers…

That's just the way it works!

Chapter 20. Train Your Thoughts

Many years ago, my family and I took our first-ever trip during the Christmas season. Since I had always worked in retail and put in long hours during December, we typically stayed home and enjoyed Chicago's lovely December weather rather than relaxing by a pool in the hot Florida sun. This year was going to be different, though, and we were all very excited to get the trip started. During the plane ride down, I read a great book on positive thinking. Little did I know how quickly it would come in handy!

As I hadn't traveled in December since I was a small child, I wasn't expecting the throng of warm-weather seekers. My family and I were shocked to see that the line at the car rental counter stretched out the door. We waited patiently (sort of) for 45 minutes, only to learn that we were at the wrong place!

Have you ever made a bone-headed move like that? Done something that left you scratching your head in disbelief? Typically, this would have thrown me for a complete loop; however, I was able to draw upon what I learned from the book I'd just read and to frame a new, positive mental attitude to save the day! *"Good news and challenging news," I told my family. "The challenge: we've been waiting all this time at the wrong car rental place! The good news is that we've been in Florida for 45 minutes, and I'm not even sunburned yet!"*

The children weren't impressed. Neither was the wife, come to think of it!

Situations in life can be framed either as positive or negative, happy or sad.

You have all heard the expression: "When life gives you lemons, make lemonade." That's how I try to live my life. One's frame of reference makes an enormous difference, and how we frame our thoughts is a choice. Had I remained upset by the car rental fiasco, it would have been my choice! It also would have been my choice to be unhappy about the long walk to the proper car rental place. However, I chose to look at the bright side of that, too – at least I got in a workout!

I was training my thoughts.

That day, I utilized a skill that we all have at our disposal but need to call upon more often. I was training my thoughts. Whether you're trying to rent a car (at the right place), earn a promotion or dive off the highest diving board at the local pool, you have the ability to train your thoughts and monitor your self-talk. How effectively you employ this skill is often the difference between success and failure. Those who *outrun ordinary and achieve extraordinary* are vigilant about their thoughts.

Let's emphasize this point again in a slightly different way because it's a critical part of your transformation: *Your success or failure in any endeavor, however large or small, will depend on your "programming" – how you internalize the words you accept from others and what you say when you talk to yourself.*

We often say or think things about ourselves as a joke (or in frustration) and don't realize just how detrimental this can be. The reason this habit is so damaging is that, as you now know, our subconscious reacts similarly to factual and fictional information. For example, let's say your son, Johnny, is upset about a poor grade on his geometry test. You want to tread lightly to keep his self-esteem intact, so you ask something seemingly innocuous such as, *"Would you like to get a tutor to help you understand the difficult concepts?"* His heated response is *"I'm a MORON, Mom…"* or *"Dad, I'm stupid. Don't waste your money…"* Of course (as your heart slowly breaks), you'll do your best to diffuse such talk by saying something like, *"Honey, everybody struggles from time to time. We'll get some help for the next test!"*

The irony of Johnny's self-talk is that it's probably not even close to being true. There could be hundreds of reasons behind his low score, including some factors that may be beyond his control. Often there is simply no justification for such harmful language and the substance of the message is merely a figment of one's misguided imagination. In spite of this (and your reassuring words), Johnny's thoughts can nevertheless cause short-term (and in some cases long-term) damage.

Yes, such random thoughts and comments may *seem* benign, but they can cause more harm than meets the eye. Think of your subconscious mind as a room full of file cabinets. In these cabinets is the sum total of your life experiences: What you've been through, what you believe and how you feel plus much, much more. It's pretty much a catalog of everything that's ever happened to you. It's all there. This is why you remember obscure facts about long-ago events and names of people you haven't seen for 20 years. It's the reason I remember most of my high school track times, although some I'd like to forget!

It's all there in the rusty file cabinets, memories good and bad, all sitting around and waiting to be called upon at some point in the future. Then comes a simple comment - *"I'm stupid!"* - and your subconscious goes to work.

The words "I'm stupid" said in jest or in a heated moment are a catalyst for a mad scramble of activity to **prove the statement true.** The mind rifles through events past and present, words spoken or heard and situations encountered in a search for supporting evidence. In addition, the brain will fire new neurons in support of the negative thought. And once that trail is blazed, it gets easier and easier to support the same ludicrous claims in the future. Moreover, the more emotional your state is while this is transpiring, the worse the effect will be. Saying, "I can't do this," while sobbing uncontrollably reinforces the new path even more quickly, and much more strongly.

Author Doug Bench sheds light on this phenomenon in his book *Revolutionize Your Brain.*

> As your neurons fire thoughts across the synapses in your brain you are creating an electrochemical pattern in your brain that influences your **health, feelings, beliefs, decisions and actions.** THOUGHTS are extremely powerful and when

you fire off a thought, it creates a new road of neuron connections. It becomes much easier to travel the new road in the future when you think the same or similar thoughts. The more you send a message down a brain pathway, the easier it becomes for it to go down that pathway again.

So in the case of Johnny, our student with the bad test score, his subconscious is put to task as soon as the negative words leave his mouth. Without him being aware that this is happening, his mind will pull anything and everything it can to prove his claim: The day he answered a question incorrectly and his classmates laughed, the last time he achieved a low score, the time he achieved a decent score but felt it was due to luck because he didn't know the material, the time he sat in class staring out the window because he couldn't follow what the teacher was saying.

Then the next time Johnny has a test, it will be much more natural for him to see failure, rather than success. This will likely hamper his ability to his ability to choose the correct answer...and stick with it.

Thoughts are inherently negative.

Ten thousand years ago, looking for the negative aspect of every situation was a survival mechanism because every single day was a struggle between life and death. The early humans who prepared for the worst were the ones who fared best. Times are obviously different now. Danger is out there but doesn't lurk around every corner like in pre-historic times. However, our thoughts still skew towards the negative.

What is the color of your thoughts?

We all have the ability to train our thoughts. What are the color of your thoughts?

One of my favorite authors on this subject is Dr. Shad Helmstetter, Ph.D., who writes and teaches about self-talk. In his book *The Power of Neuroplasticity*, Shad talks about how we all have the potential to "color" our thoughts. Imagine a piece of paper showing an outline of a human brain. Now think about holding in your hands a bright crayon and a dark crayon. (I suggest yellow and grey). With that image in mind, consider Shad's words:

> There are different views on how many thoughts each of us thinks in a day; estimates range from 12,500 to 70,000 or more. For purposes of coloring in our brain picture, we'll use the number 35,000 as the number of individual thoughts each of us has in a day. That would mean you'd have to make 35,000 colored marks on your brain picture in one day. (Big job!) At the end of the first day, how would your picture look? If you had actually colored in everything you said, and every thought you thought, yellow for a positive thought and grey for a negative thought, what color would your brain picture show the most?
>
> Imagine doing that for a month. Then imagine doing it for a year. At the end of a year, if you had marked in a color that represented everything you said and every thought you thought, what color would your brain picture be?

I do this exercise with my training groups. It's often a challenge to convince people that they get to choose the color of their thoughts, just as they get to choose the color of their crayon.

Now that we know how important thoughts are, here are a few ways to transform yours:

- **Monitor your self-talk** – get an idea of what you're thinking and saying.

  It's easy for someone to tell you to eliminate all negative self-talk, but that's not possible. Moreover, it's not really a question of eliminating negative thoughts; it's more about turning those thoughts around and dispelling the untrue notions that much of your self-talk is built upon. It starts with simply being more cognizant. Listen, monitor and become more aware of what you say to yourself, not just when things are bad, but also when things are going well.

  Capture your first thoughts when you wake up in the morning. Are you eager to face the day, or is getting out of bed the last thing you want to do? Continue to capture your thoughts as the day progresses. Consider your thoughts when you're with friends, family, colleagues, etc., and also while you're alone.

Once again, the must-read book *The Power of Neuroplasticity*, offers guidance:

> Listening to your own self-talk is part of mindfulness; your own self-talk is something you should be aware of at all times. To learn what your own programs really look like, monitor what you say out loud, but also monitor what you say or think silently to yourself. (In self-talk, your thoughts are as powerful as your spoken words.)

Pay particular attention to negative limiting thoughts - statements like *"I'm going to flunk this test"* or *"There's no way I can make that sale"* or *"I'm afraid to ask my customer that question."* Listen for pretty much any statement that suggests that you're not capable of doing what you're setting out to do.

Then, reframe the thought in a more objective way. Rewrite the language because your next thought will have an effect on your mind, as described earlier. Come up with something positive and productive. If you're afraid of asking your customer a question, instead of thinking something negative, focus on how you can ask the question in a manner that will yield a good answer.

- **Choose your words more positively** – feed your mind the nourishment it needs to be successful.

One theme I've tried to outline in this book is that every thought and image matters. Many people believe in the law of attraction, which asserts that "like attracts like" and that by focusing on positive or negative thoughts, one can bring about positive or negative results. I agree to a certain extent. The winter of 2014 has been brutally cold and icy in Chicago. When my son Danny goes running, instead of telling him to watch for ice, I tell him to make sure to find the dry pavement. If I don't want him to slip on the ice (and break his wrist…again), why should I put that visual out there?

Similarly, I don't believe in saying *good news and bad news*. I'd rather say *good news and challenging news*. In truth, most people are fortunate and don't deal with truly bad news on a daily basis. They deal with challenging news, much of which causes worry about things that probably won't happen anyway. Why label it with a negative word such as *bad*?

- **Generate enthusiasm** – have a great sense of expectancy each day.

When my dad and I started running together when I was very young, he made sure to generate some enthusiasm before our first run. We made a special trip to buy the proper attire and footwear, but, more important, we spent an evening together talking about running. Dad wasn't dwelling on the fact that Mom was forcing him to quit smoking and get in shape. He wanted both of us to be excited and enthusiastic about our new endeavor.

Every once in a while someone will say, "I'm just not that enthusiastic!" In response, I'll ask, "Well, how did you react when your baby daughter started walking? Did you clap like you were at a polo match or did you hoot and holler?" The answer is obvious. We all have the ability to generate enthusiasm. It's a choice!

- **See the positive in things** - don't dwell on the negative.

The tendency in life and business is to push positive things to the background and to dwell instead on negative events and occurrences. I remember having a manager working for me who would always complain when an order was filled incorrectly. Of course, I knew that it was important to learn why the problem was occurring and to fix it; however, I always took time to notice and compliment my team on the good things that were happening. I wanted them to remember all the orders that were completed *successfully* and to take pride in their accomplishments.

Be sure to learn from the negatives, but always take note of the positives, as well. If you do this, there's a greater chance that you'll continue your productive behaviors!

- **Demonstrate positive body language** – check your body language to ensure sure that your physical actions are consistent with your improved thoughts.

Demonstrate your positive attitude through your body language. Let others see your smile. Smiling shows warmth and indicates that you are an open and accepting person. Plus, it's actually good for you! The act of smiling induces the release of neurotransmitters in the brain that produce feelings of happiness.

Also focus on speaking sincerely to people when you greet them, whether on the phone or in person. Try this: the next time you run into someone that you haven't seen in a while, show through your actions (your smile, tone of voice, choice of words) that you're genuinely happy to see that person. Trust me, it will make a hugely positive impression.

Really, when you think about it, nearly every success in life (and certainly every success portrayed in this book) involves an element of individuals *training their thoughts*. My purpose in this chapter was to share some of the science behind this phenomenon.

We've learned more about how the mind works in the last 20 years than in all prior years combined. Those of you who use this knowledge to your advantage will be in a much better position to *outrun ordinary and achieve extraordinary.*

That's just the way it works!

The Finish

Like most teenagers, I had posters plastered all over the walls of my bedroom. However, instead of the lovely Farrah Fawcett or rock groups such as AC/DC and Iron Maiden, the images on my posters all had something to do with running.

My favorite was a Nike poster titled *"There is no finish line."* This poster depicted a long, desolate, hilly road in the middle of farm country with just one solitary runner seemingly alone with his thoughts. You could see from the picture that the road went on for miles and miles, and I interpreted the message to mean that you can always continue running, achieving, growing, developing and succeeding.

You may be thinking: Darryl, is there a finish line or not?

I hear you. The answer is both *yes and no*!

I'll explain. To me, the finish line symbolizes accomplishing a goal. Perhaps the goal is empowering women (Sheira MacKenzie's goal) or being able to run every day (one of Melissa Engel's goals). Whatever the case, once an objective is completed, it's reasonable to think of some sort of "finish line" being crossed.

However, viewed through another lens – that of continuous growth and improvement – there really is no hard and fast finish line. After all, it's not as though once Sheira empowers a room full of women or Melissa runs her next half-marathon, either one of these impressive women will stop achieving!

Accomplishing a goal does not necessarily mean that you've *outrun ordinary*. Your story doesn't end there, and because of that, you're likely to often find yourself in those middle miles I have spoken about (the part of the race where the excitement of the start has faded and you can't imagine the glory of the finish line) - that place I hope you feel more confident navigating now that you have read this book.

In *See You at the Finish Line,* I've shared 20 keys to help you *outrun ordinary and achieve extraordinary*. We looked at a variety of success principles, one at a time, and now I'd like to share an example of how the pieces fit together to drive meaningful change. To illustrate, I will tell you about Danny, my middle son, who (as you know by now) is a high school runner.

Danny has more determination in his big toe than I have in my entire body. He's my running hero! In my view, he's already *outrun ordinary and achieved extraordinary* for two reasons. First, he never gives up. He never quits races and he never takes a practice off. Period. Second, he maximizes his potential by never giving less than 100% effort, something that I never did as a runner. But for Danny to accomplish this much, he had to change something significant.

He had to radically change his breathing habits.

Danny began his running career just last year. It was very slow going at first (in part because his previous hobbies had been playing video games and eating pizza). When he ran, he always looked like he was in some form of discomfort. In fact, you could hear him hyperventilating from what seemed like a mile away. It sounded like a freight train coming, and when the race ended, it took a long time before he was feeling normal again.

While his run times were hitting rock bottom, his frustration was skyrocketing. At first, our pediatrician suspected a form of exercise-induced asthma, but an inhaler and other measures were of no benefit. So, before the cross country season started in August, we resolved to get some answers.

It turned out that Danny had a condition called Vocal Cord Dysfunction, which was causing the airway near his throat to close when he exerted himself. No wonder he was gasping for air the way he was! The doctor advised us of two treatment options, the first being surgery and the second making fundamental changes to the way Danny breathed.

We opted for the second option and found a breathing coach to work with Danny. This, combined with Danny's use of many of the strategies outlined this book, enabled him to bring about a dramatic change in his performance.

Here's what he did: Danny *embraced the race*. He believed that changing his breathing was possible, when honestly, I wasn't so sure. The changes required seemed so extensive (in essence, relearning how to breathe), but Danny's belief never wavered. He also *trained his thoughts* by changing his inner dialogue.

As you might imagine, it's a challenge to get solid information from a 16-year-old, but I'm fairly certain he tried to eliminate his negative self-talk, a task made more difficult by the fact that the season had started and his first few meets hadn't gone very well.

But, still, even with these early disappointments, he was able to *get back up* and continue to race hard. The situation was the epitome of the middle miles. His times were actually getting slower because he was trying so hard to adopt the new way of breathing. He was in no-man's-land.

During this difficult time, Danny had every right to compare himself to his teammates, but he was sure to *run his own race.* His goal was that his breathing would be better today than it was yesterday, and even better tomorrow. He *exercised his voice* by asking me to take him back for additional sessions with the breathing coach, and he *stayed on course* by requesting (and accepting) that individual's feedback. Most importantly, he *dismissed the doubts.* He trusted that his efforts would lead to success, so he completed the suggested exercises religiously, even during the early stages, when his pessimism was probably at its highest.

And it worked.

His breathing is great now. In fact, he almost won a race the other day. It was a race so exciting, I believe I may have acted like a teenage girl at a Justin Bieber concert. I'm not sure… we'll have to watch the video!

Here's what I am sure of: If you follow what I've outlined in this book and use my stories and the stories of the individuals profiled as inspiration, you will *outrun ordinary and achieve extraordinary.*

That's just the way it works!

About the Author

Darryl Rosen speaks, trains, coaches and writes on the subjects of success, sales, management, and customer service. He is an experienced business professional, having formerly served as President and Owner of Sam's Wines & Spirits, a $70 million multi-store retailer in the Chicago area.

Through his transformational keynotes, workshops and coaching sessions, he's helped the professionals of numerous organizations *outrun ordinary and achieve extraordinary*.

He is passionate about sharing what his experience has taught him about the topics of motivation, excellence in execution, and achievement. His favorite way of illustrating these lessons is through engaging stories and analogies. His audiences consistently find him to be entertaining as well as informative!

Darryl earned an MBA in Marketing and Organizational Behavior from Northwestern University's Kellogg School of Management. He also holds a Bachelor's Degree in Accounting from Indiana University and is a Certified Public Accountant.

When he is not working, Darryl enjoys running (he has completed 14 marathons) and spending time with his wife and three sons. He is also a strong supporter of philanthropic efforts dedicated to improving the lives of children.

For information about how Darryl can bring his messages alive for you or your team, contact him by visiting www.darrylrosen.com.

Other Books by Darryl Rosen

Surviving the Middle Miles
26.2 Ways to Cross the Finish Line with
　Your Customers

Winning the Customer Loyalty Marathon
How to Achieve Sales and Service
Excellence in the Beverage Business

Unleashing Your Inner Sales Coach
　How to Inspire, Motivate and "Coach"
　Your Sales Team to Success

Table for Three? Bringing Your Smart
Phone to Lunch & 50 Dumb Mistakes
Great Managers Don't Make!

Cornering Sales Success
　How to Use the Intersection of Facts and
　Relationships to Increase Sales and
　Broaden Distribution